Close Relationships

Marie-Louise von Franz, Honorary Patron

**Studies in Jungian Psychology
by Jungian Analysts**

Daryl Sharp, General Editor

Close Relationships

Family, Friendship, Marriage

Eleanor Bertine, M.D.

Foreword by Edward F. Edinger

This volume is an edited reprint of *Human Relationships: In the Family, In Friendship, in Love,* © 1958 by Eleanor Bertine.

Canadian Cataloguing in Publication Data

Bertine, Eleanor, 1887-1968
  Close relationships

(Studies in Jungian psychology by Jungian analysts; 57)

Originally published (1958) under title: Human relationships:
in the family, in friendship, in love.

Includes bibliographical references and index.

ISBN 0-919123-58-9

1. Interpersonal relations.   2. Interpersonal communication.
3. Jung, C.G. (Carl Gustav), 1875-1961. I. Title. II. Title:
Human relationships: in the family, in friendship, in love.
III. Series.

BF636.B47 1992   158'.2   C92-094357-8

INNER CITY BOOKS
Box 1271, Station Q, Toronto, Canada M4T 2P4
Telephone (416) 927-0355
FAX 416-924-1814

Honorary Patron: Marie-Louise von Franz.
Publisher and General Editor: Daryl Sharp.
Senior Editor: Victoria Cowan.

INNER CITY BOOKS was founded in 1980 to promote the
understanding and practical application of the work of C.G. Jung.

Cover: Spiritual Sun Birds, by Canadian artist Clemence Wescoope.

Index by Daryl Sharp

Printed and bound in Canada by John Deyell Company Limited.

Contents

See final page for other titles by Inner City Books

Eleanor Bertine
(Photo by Marian Lockwood)

Foreword

Anyone who makes a serious effort to understand Jung's work cannot fail to be amazed at the magnitude of the man. Although he died more than thirty years ago, the impact of his discoveries concerning the nature of the psyche has scarcely begun to be felt beyond the consulting room. The breadth and depth of his view are staggering and for this reason many shy away from further investigation. Such a man needs intermediaries to communicate his revolutionary insights in more personal forms.

Eleanor Bertine was among the first to perform this mediating function. She did so not only in her writing, but also by exemplifying in her life and personality the impact Jung had on one intelligent professional living in our age of transition.

Eleanor Bertine was a pioneer, one of that scant handful of people who first brought analytical psychology to America. Born in 1887 in New York, she graduated from Vassar College and completed her medical training in 1908 at the Cornell College of Medicine. In 1920 she went to London where she attended a seminar by Jung and thereafter worked with him in Zürich for protracted periods of time. Together with M. Esther Harding and Kristine Mann she was a founding member of the Analytical Psychology Club of New York in 1936.[1] She became a patron of the C.G. Jung Institute in Zürich when it was founded in 1948 and in 1962 of the C.G. Jung Foundation established in New York.

I knew Eleanor Bertine first as the friend and partner of my analyst, Esther Harding. Later I knew her as my control analyst and still later as a professional colleague. What first impressed me was the clarity and agility of her mind. She had an unusual capacity to recog-

---

[1] [This impressive trio shared a summer house on Bailey Island in Maine, where the now-legendary Bailey Island seminars took place in the thirties. One of these was specifically organized for Jung on his visit to America in 1936. M. Esther Harding is widely known for her seminal books, including *The Way of All Women* and *Woman's Mysteries.* Kristine Mann's legacy was the basis of the Kristine Mann Library of the Analytical Psychology Club of New York.—Ed.]

7

nize the essential issues in a situation and to give them concise expression. As I got to know her better, other qualities stood out more prominently: her integrity and her empathy. Although she was capable of taking quite firm positions, she was always willing to examine matters openly in a mutual quest for the objective truth.

In no other field except religion does it make so much difference to one's personal life what theory one affirms. The soul may be nourished or killed, cramped or inundated, depending on what theory of the psyche one holds. Furthermore, different theories may be needed by different individuals and at different stages of conscious development. Hence every presentation is to some extent a subjective confession. It is one of the virtues of this author that she recognized the subjective factor and allowed it overt expression.

"Ars totum requirit hominem"—the art requires the whole person. This old alchemical saying epitomized Jung's approach to the art of psychotherapy. Eleanor Bertine followed this principle. In this book the reader is granted a rare opportunity for contact with a wise and ample personality. Here the reader will find sound feeling side by side with clear thinking; a respect for facts combined with an awareness of hidden meanings; a warm, personal candor that yet remains quite objective.

Although Eleanor Bertine was a medical doctor, she did not succumb to the clinician's tendency to see the patient only in the categories of pathology. She was aware that all the vicissitudes of personal life, no matter how trivial or sordid they may seem, contain a latent value if one can approach them correctly. In her own words, "Any human experience may be a maze in which to wander to destruction or a laboratory for the creation of consciousness, depending on the way it is met."[2]

Eleanor Bertine committed herself to the life task of creating consciousness, both in herself and in others. The integrity and devotion she brought to this task shine through in this book.

Edward F. Edinger
Los Angeles

---

[2] *Jung's Contribution to Our Time: The Collected Papers of Eleanor Bertine,* ed. Elizabeth C. Rohrbach (New York: The C.G. Jung Foundation for Analytical Psychology, 1967), p. 30.

Introduction

The analytic method of C.G. Jung is really an education in depth quite as much as it is a form of psychotherapy. Therefore those whom it attracts are often by no means abnormal but are seeking a fuller, more meaningful life through psychological enlightenment.

Some problem of human relationship is the immediate cause which brings many people to consult an analyst. In the privacy of the consulting room a multitude of such difficulties are revealed. Whether the relation is one of friend, lover, business associate or enemy, it has the power to bring joy, sorrow, anxiety and despair.

The stories are quite familiar. A daughter can't get along with her mother, a marriage is on the rocks, a man smarts under the overbearing domination of his boss, and, as a consequence, life is filed with bitterness and resentment. These are not good companions to live with and anyone possessed by them needs to be released. But, it may be said, all this is a matter of psychological development. If you are mature, you can handle the problem. If not, no attempt to learn how from the top of the head would be of the least use. So let the analyst concentrate on getting on with the analysis, and let the patient handle outside problems in the meantime.

Of course, I agree one hundred per cent with the first half of this proposition, that is, that the quality of a relationship reflects the stage of development of the participants. But just as an improved capacity to relate is one outcome of psychological development, so also development itself may be accelerated by sincere work on relationships and the unconscious factors that influence them. Actually, getting on with the analysis may require getting on with the relationship. For, to a young or unconscious person, the view of, and consequently the reaction to, the outer world, and especially to other people, is distorted by projections of his or her own psychological contents, which then seem to belong to the other person. This condition renders mutual understanding impossible and makes for so much trouble that one may be driven to realize and assimilate projections, thus greatly extending the area of consciousness.

Whenever there is a very intense reaction to someone or something there will be found a projection at the bottom of it, a projection not only from the personal life, such as the qualities or characteristics of one's mother, but also from the archetypes of the deep or collective unconscious.[3] For instance, if a youth sees a pair of pretty ankles, the biological instinct of sex may be stimulated. But at the same time a number of psychological reactions are likely to take place which may reflect not only his personal relations with girls, but also the collective reactions men have had to women down through the ages. The stirring of such images is responsible for the glamour of romance or the fear of the woman and her power to captivate and exploit. Thus, his feelings in the particular situation may have very little to do with the real girl who confronts him. Symbols of these archetypes might be Aphrodite or Helen of Troy, on the one hand, expressing the lure, or the lorelei or *la belle dame sans merci* on the other, expressing the threat.

The massive libido[4] charge of an instinctual or archetypal experience is most important in the process of becoming conscious, for libido is energy and psychological development takes enormous energy. Sometimes this is generated within analysis in the form of intense inner happenings or projections onto the person of the analyst in the experience of transference.[5] But at other times this has been constellated outside the analytic situation: a youth is called to war, a loved one dies, serious illness strikes, or the patient has fallen in love. Here is emotion, the raw dynamic of life, which is essential for

---

[3] [Jung described archetypes as primordial and inherited structural elements of the human psyche, "systems of readiness for action, and at the same time images and emotions." ("Mind and Earth," *Civilization in Transition,* CW 10, par. 53). [CW refers throughout to *The Collected Works of C.G. Jung* (Bollingen Series XX), 20 vols., trans. R.F.C. Hull, ed. H. Read, M. Fordham, G. Adler, Wm. McGuire; Princeton: Princeton University Press, 1953-1979]

[4] The word *libido,* according to Jung's usage, is not limited to sexuality as it is with Freud, but refers to psychic energy in general.

[5] Transference is the projection upon another person of emotionally tinged contents, thereby producing an unreal relationship involving undue dependence. It occurs most frequently, though by no means exclusively, in the relation of the patient to the analyst. Here the conscious work upon the ensuing situation is an important way of assimilating the projected unconscious contents, thereby releasing one from the blind spots which interfere with all relationships.

progress. One cannot steer a boat that has no means of propulsion. There is little transformation in a cold retort. So wherever this precious stuff of life is produced, it may be used for the objective of psychological transformation.

Human relationship, even if the experience is one of frustration, is probably the greatest generator of intense libido. This has a nonpersonal element, which is archetypal, in spite of having arisen at the very core of the most personal experience. Charles Morgan wrote a book some years ago called *Sparkenbroke*, in which the hero, a poet, in searching to discover what the sources of this experience in depth are, came to the conclusion that it is brought about by three things: love, the impact of death and the creative act, especially in poetry, for that was his field, but also more generally in any creative art.

In any problem that arouses the emotional depths, good advice is quite useless, for the way to proceed should be the expression of the individual's uniqueness, not of an opinion borrowed from somebody else. To find the individual way requires contact with the unconscious. However, it sometimes happens that a person seems to have no capacity at all for even glimpsing the reality and importance of the unconscious, especially, though not necessarily, if young and extraverted. His or her interest flows exclusively outward, and one almost despairs of being able to touch anything at a deeper level. Then a dream about relationship, whose emotional content cannot be evaded, may make such an impression that it brings the analysis vividly to life and affects the dreamer's entire future.

An excellent example of this occurs to me. It was the case of a young woman in her early twenties, an artist, gifted in her work, pretty, attractive, gay and happy-go-lucky. She had lots of suitors, but much preferred to keep them in that capacity rather than settle down with any one of them. But then she met a man who was her polar opposite, introverted, intense, demanding and altogether difficult. And he wanted to marry her. She tried to put him off, so he sent her to me! She was smart enough to realize quickly that she had to choose between playing around with the many and losing the one, whom she liked, incidentally, much the best, or marrying the one and giving up the many.

She chose according to her heart, with the proviso, however, that she should continue her painting as before. But, as usual, *l'homme propose et Dieu dispose*. She immediately became pregnant, against her firmest intentions. This time she came back to see me under her own steam. She felt caught, trapped, forced to become a responsible woman when she wanted so badly a few more years of carefree Bohemian existence. Her impulse was all in favor of getting rid of the problem by an induced abortion. Not having any connection with the unconscious, she had no idea how such an act often sets a woman against her instinctive nature, and how terribly nature can strike back. I talked with her about the seriousness of that decision without producing much of an impression, so I suggested she earnestly ask her unconscious to give her some guidance in a dream. She hadn't much hope of that, for dreams meant nothing to her, but agreed to try.

Sure enough, next time she came to her hour of analysis with what she called a silly little fragment. This was it: She dreamed she saw an enormous elephant, much larger than a real one. It was walking westward with a slow deliberate pace right across the continent from the Atlantic to the Pacific. When it arrived at the rim of the sea, the sun was just about to drop beneath the horizon. She saw the great creature outlined against the red ball of the sun, at the edge of the vast western ocean.

Though she tried to laugh off the dream, it had obviously impressed her. And no wonder, for it was the intrusion of contents from the archetypal depths into her too personal and childish existence. I asked for associations. She spoke of seeing elephants in the zoo, of their massive size and earthiness, as though they were hunks of the earth itself walking about. Westward was in the direction of the sun's journey. "Going west" was a current phrase for dying. The sun was the giver of light. The edge of the ocean was the border of the unknown, where one couldn't go any farther, and the setting sun was also the death of the day. So this archetypal elephant is incarnated reality, life in the flesh, and it goes inexorably along the path of the sun. Thus, the ordained paths of the body and the spirit parallel each other. To deviate by rejecting her pregnancy would be to break the law of this correspondence, to bring disorder into the picture. Her feeling, rather than her thinking, repudiated such a thing. She felt that she simply could not interfere with the sunwise movement of life just to suit her personal convenience or pleasure.

Thus the dream, which on the extraverted side related to her husband and prospective baby, on the other side, the introverted, gave a highly philosophical representation of the lines of force of the psyche and the laws that rule the inner being. It was more than she could take in at the stage of development she had up to that time attained, but it stayed with her and has been a sort of talisman through her subsequent life. The anticipated baby is now grown, and the marriage, which had promised right along to be difficult, has amply justified this expectation. But she has stood by loyally through thick and thin, and has finally brought her family and herself to some measure of the contentment that is always the result of worked-out problems. Naturally she has had a good deal of analysis in the course of the years. But it was this relatedness problem that opened the way to the inner life, made her analysis "take," and led to the maturing of an exceedingly fine woman.

Individuation cannot take place in a vacuum. As Jung once said, "The hermit either will be flooded by the unconscious or he will become a very dull fellow." Life must be lived to the full if it is to change anyone for the better. It is possible to develop a certain amount of consciousness in relation to things and inanimate nature, and even more in relation to animals, where feeling may be strongly touched. But only another human being can constellate so many sides of ourselves, can react so pointedly, and can bring to consciousness so much of which we had been unaware. And because of the real values involved and the consequently keen desires, the heat of emotion is raised high enough to produce the transformation more readily and more often in relationship than in almost any other experience of life.

Sometimes it is even possible to follow in a single relationship the transformation of the libido from one stage of development to the next, as symbolized in the chakra system of Kundalini, or tantric yoga.[6] Here the nonpersonal libido is conceived of as the feminine counterpart of the god Shiva, who lies coiled up, asleep in the pelvic basin, in the form of the serpent Kundalini. This lasts for as long as the state of purely personal consciousness, which the Hindu calls unconsciousness, persists. The attempt of this yoga is to awaken Kundalini and to force her to rise through the narrow passage of the

---

[6] See Arthur Avalon, *The Serpent Power* (Madras: Ganesh & Co., 1931).

spinal canal, Shushumna, thus passing through the various chakras (which are really mandalas symbolizing the successive levels of consciousness)[7] until she reaches Sahasrara, at the very crown of the head, where she unites with her lord Shiva.

The following example, which occurred in the course of a relationship, is a parallel to this yogic development. It concerns a woman who, in connection with her work, met a man to whom she was much attracted. She was a stranger in the city and lonely, and the man's companionship seemed to be the answer to "a maiden's prayer." He would take her out, dance with her, occupy her evenings and many weekends. All this was a matter of her merely personal libido, manageable, pleasant, but quite cold-blooded. However, it was in the direction of the life process and she thrived on it. The gods, here the archetypes and instincts, were back of it. This stage of consciousness would correspond to the lowest chakra, Muladhara.

The attraction soon increased and became definitely erotic. She found herself jealous of the other women he was seeing, wanting more and more time and attention from him. She realized she was getting deeply involved. She had fallen into Svadisthana, the water region, where live the images of the forces of the unconscious, and was in danger of being devoured by the Macara, the great serpent dragon, which is its characterizing symbol. This would mean a complete domination by the night aspect of the unconscious. She would become prey to the desirousness not only of instinct, but also of all the powerful archetypes of satisfaction that cluster around the opposite sex, such as functioning socially and otherwise as one of a couple—marriage, home and family.

This overwhelming, cold-blooded desirousness quickly lit the fire of passion. Hot emotion came up to accompany, and partly replace, desire. The libido had now reached Manipura, the fire region, presided over by the violent sun ram. Yet it is called the place of jew-

---

[7] A mandala is a symbolic diagram, usually in the form of a circle or square, or a combination of the two. It may be a prescribed ritualistic pattern or be made by the individual. In either case, it is an attempt to find a pictured reconciliation of divergent elements within an ordered whole. It is used in the Orient as a basis for meditation, and frequently occurs in drawings of those in analysis. See "Commentary on 'The Secret of the Golden Flower,' " *Alchemical Studies,* CW 13.

els, for the intensity resulting from the strong constellation of opposites is the heaping up of life, with all its potentiality for good and ill. The conflict was especially severe because the young man, though most friendly and agreeable, seemed to have no thought of anything more than the existing platonic situation. So she had to be her own battlefield, contain her own tumult.

Then he went away on business for several months. On his return he announced his engagement to another woman. That was a stunning blow. On the surface she took it very well, but, in the silence of the night, she had it out with herself. The storm raged in her for weeks. Finally she wrote me:

> Oh this unbearable pain! But no, not unbearable now. I managed to pull myself together last night and have been able to work well today. It was all pain on one level, a crucifixion of the personal life. But at the same moment, I had also the actual experience of the bringing together, the sharp focusing of the Self in a great suffering, tantamount to a great joy. I can feel how, at that depth, it really makes no difference whether the experience that brings Self-realization is one of grief or joy. There flames up an intensity, an ecstasy, which is far beyond the personal. But the all-too-human woman still remains in me too, and she still cries out in her pain, "I feel as though I had conceived and my baby is an abortion. It dies without having lived. Life passes me by and leaves me out, set apart, not up to the business of living, and so accurst." Then the other voice comes back, "This experience has given you a glimpse of something greater than anything the outer world can give, even at its most radiant best. It can be yours to make it a living reality."

This is a typical experience of the next chakra, Anahata, in which Ishvara, a symbol of the Self,[8] is first glimpsed as a shy antelope at the edge of the forest. Sometimes it will come near, and then with a bound it will be gone. It is evident from this bit of her letter how far this woman went in her inner development, led, or perhaps I should say forced, by the psychological process set in motion by a love affair that was almost entirely one-sided.

---

[8] The term Self as used by Jung stands for the totality of the psyche. It is both the archetype of wholeness and the regulating center of the personality. "It might equally well be called the 'God within us.' " ("The Mana-Personality," *Two Essays on Analytical Psychology,* CW 7, par. 399)

The character of the inner movement from level to level is archetypal, as well as are the images on the way. Yet to the eye of the ordinary person, the whole thing would have appeared as a rather humiliating comedy. The expression in meaningful form of these archetypes underlying human life is the great function of the artist. But to relate rightly to them in reality is the meaning of the human enterprise. And this will be fought out to a very large extent in the arena of human relationships—the battle of the gods and the demons may take place in the course of an apparently personal conversation between John and Mary.

It is in the hope of clarifying the way these archetypes enter into daily life that I have chosen to write about interpersonal relationships. They are the most subtle, the most complicated, and, for the majority of people, probably the most frequent and moving setting in which the awe-inspiring archetypes of the unconscious are experienced. And finally, they stimulate the process of growth, which, while it aims at a deeper, more satisfying connection with another human being, actually leads into the path of individuation, which is the finding of the Self.

1
The Family

The earliest archetypes to present themselves are those of the family, the mother and the father, though their approach is entirely unconscious. We are apt to think that the individual comes first and then feels joined to the family. But psychologically it doesn't happen that way. The family, as Jung has aptly put it, is like the primordial soup in which the individuals swim around as little fishes, incapable of living apart.

The family is taken for granted by the child as the necessary background which is there as a matter of course. It predates the separate members who compose it, and appears to each newcomer simply as the way things are. Outsiders are potentially dangerous, but the family never repudiates the child, no matter how it acts. It feels that the family's love does not have to be earned, any more than the stomach has to earn the loyalty of the liver. The family stands together against anything inimical in the outside world. We not only assume this will be true, but take it as our right.

I remember a young woman tied to her family by a peculiarly tough umbilical cord. She was an adored and thoroughly spoiled daughter of rather elderly parents who had made her the shining center of their lives. She had recently married and wasn't happy. Her attitude toward marriage was utterly childish, as was what she expected from analysis. I was somewhat reserved and let her do the talking. Presently she stopped and looked over at me suspiciously, saying, "I don't think you like me very much!" She had been talking like a selfish little brat, but still she took it for granted that she should already be teacher's pet, even with someone almost a stranger. Very quietly I asked her what the person in the room with me was presenting for me to like. This detachment was too much for her, and she soon dropped off, as I had anticipated she would. She simply could not function unless an admiring parental audience was responding properly to the show she was putting on.

Another tragic illustration of a regressive bondage to the family

17

was given me by a patient in the medical clinic of the university from which I got my degree. This was before I was an analyst, when I was practicing general medicine. She was a young woman in her late twenties. She seemed generally to be going to pieces; she was nervous, jittery, couldn't sleep, couldn't eat, couldn't concentrate, and feared she would lose her job and her mind as a consequence. A thorough physical examination revealed no adequate explanation, so I asked her about the conditions of her life. Here is what she told me.

She was the eldest of a family of eleven children. The father was dead and the mother an overworked, complaining creature who screamed at the children but had not the slightest control over them. They all lived in a tenement of three tiny rooms. They were desperately poor and the atmosphere was one of constant quarreling and vituperation. The patient was the main support of all this rabble, though the mother and the older boys did a little outside work when there was time and they could get it.

This story was enough to account for any nervous breakdown, so I suggested she get a little place for herself and only eat at home. She said she couldn't possibly afford it because the family took all her earnings. I asked if they also would not be better off if she gave what she could and let them apply for some help from one of the charitable associations to supplement it, rather than for her to break down completely and have to be a burden instead of a support. Then she came out with the incredible truth: she could not face leaving home. She said, "We are all like that. None of us can bear being away from home, however unhappy we are there. My brother tried it last year, he signed on to a tramp steamer going down to the Caribbean. A few months later we got a little bundle of his things and a note to my mother. He said, 'I can't stand it any longer, living away from home. I'm going overboard.' So you see, I've got to stay."

Obviously this sort of fixation makes it impossible to adapt to the outside world. It is as though the individual were a dismembered part, a leg, for example, trying to make contact with whole people, for everybody else always seems to be whole under these circumstances. Outsiders are forever strangers and suspect, and must be met with power rather than love, even when friends are desperately wanted. Such a person *has* to dominate, or suffer crushing defeat.

A boy of this sort was absolutely unable to finish a race if he lost the lead. He had to win or something quite against his will compelled him to drop out. He simply could not trust his fellows to see his failure, so had to pretend he didn't care to win. The trouble was not an overweening ego ambition but deep insecurity. His father was psychotic, so had not been able to carry for the boy the kind of masculine power and authority which would have been an example of manliness, and in compensation the boy had become his mother's pet. So he had no satisfactory way of maintaining his ego at a stage when ego development is most important.[9] Consequently, whenever a situation threatened to expose his insecurity, he could not meet it straight but could only pull wires to hide his weakness, lest he be wiped entirely off the map.

The child lives in a state of original identity, which means it exists only as an organic part of a greater whole, the family. In this condition we see reflected symbolically the natural and right relation of the ego to the Self, but in projected form, being in the outer world instead of the inner. The parts of the psyche which are not realized as such have to be experienced as other people, to whom the child is, as a result, unconditionally bound. This is inevitable and even necessary to survival in the early stages of development, for the ego by itself is too small and weak to hold its own in the face of the overpowering aspects of reality. The words of the poet Henley often sound like a little boy whistling in the dark to keep his courage up: "I am the master of my fate: I am the captain of my soul." Haven't we all been in situations in which we recognize this attitude for what it is, a reckless inflation? The ego must find something larger and stronger than itself

---

[9] As is now well known, the ego is only a small, though significant, part of the whole psyche. Jung defines the ego as the subject of the conscious personality. It is what one means in saying "I." The Self, on the other hand, comprises the totality, both known and unknown, in which this smaller self is contained. As the goal of every form of life is to fulfill the whole of its potential, even if this striving is unconscious, so the individual psyche, whether one realizes it or not, is drawn toward the center which represents completeness. This is not theory but the actual experience of any analyst who is able to take a cooperative patient to a deep enough level of the collective unconscious. Selfhood, which Jung speaks of as a condition of individuation, necessarily involves the conscious as well as the unconscious, and so cannot be attained without the disciplined cooperation of the conscious ego, which is yet powerless to produce it alone or by its own self-will. See *Two Essays on Analytical Psychology,* CW 7.

within, or else it will remain a mere isolated fragment, crying for somebody outside who might be able to complete it.

It is small wonder that the parents tower as gods in the little world of the family. I have often been amazed at the glowing, almost numinous picture that some patients paint of parents who, in reality, came very far from justifying it. In several instances I remember women, otherwise intelligent and gifted, who described their mothers as wonderful, outstanding people, though they were in fact alcoholics whom the patients, even as children, had had to protect from making a public scandal. The quality of their descriptions was so alive that it could not be ascribed to a conscious covering up of heartbreak. An almost magical aura shone through the words, absent from their accounts of other people. The archetypal gods roared or glowed from behind the parents, even though they were pitifully inadequate carriers. And, as is so often the case, the recognition of the truth half hidden behind the projection does not necessarily affect the emotional power constellated by the presence of the archetype.

In the lives of ordinary individuals, the archetype that is the first, the most familiar, the most heart warming or most repellent, and altogether the most fateful, is that of the mother. She is closer by far than the father in the external life of the infant. Every day its comfort, well-being and very survival depend upon her, while its connection with the father is practically invisible. She keeps it warm and dry, she assuages its hunger and thirst, and its every need and every desire is nearer to her than her own. And it is not only physically that she is the comforter. She surrounds the child with tenderness and love, making an atmosphere of security in which it can trust its own efforts, try its own wings.

The maternal libido lavished on the young is a matter of the utmost psychological importance for future development. Again and again I have seen grown people with feelings so shy as to be practically frozen, yearning for close human contact but utterly unable to make a move and even scaring off any approach by their apparently unresponsive coldness. Yet this condition was actually the result of a childhood in which no love had been given, sometimes because the mother was too selfish or neurotic or otherwise emotionally crippled, and sometimes because she was dead. The son or daughter who never could go to mother with a hurt, sure of sympathy and help, or jump into mother's lap with a spontaneity in which love and joy and a lusty sense of general well-being were all mixed up, and find from her a warm if quiet response, this child has learned to keep its feelings bottled up so as not to risk the pain and even real crippling that can come from a cold or snubbing rejoinder.

The emotional injury from the absence of a mother's love was evident in a man who came to me some years ago. On the surface you would say he was a successful, well-adjusted person, for he was a judge, married and standing well in the community. But behind this facade the picture was utterly different. His marriage was unhappy, for he was homosexual with a penchant for young boys (he himself was well over fifty) whom he took under his wing, like an old hen. He protected them, spoiled them, gave them money, indeed was far too generous, and then was hurt to the quick when they deceived or exploited him and then deserted him.

Other than with these boys he had no relationships that held any emotional content whatever. He projected his extremely undeveloped affective nature onto his protégés, and then gave them the mothering he had so sorely missed. For his history was that his mother had died when he was only two years old, too soon for him to have retained any recollection of her at all, or to have experienced any grief for her death. It had never occurred to him that this loss was playing a grim role in his life. Yet early in his analysis, when a dream brought it into consciousness, he lay awake all night sobbing for the mother he had never known.

I would like to tell you that he made a fine mother transference onto me, and, by this means, worked himself up to his proper emotional age. But alas! it does not always happen like that, and it did not in this case. It was natural that his relation to me was ambivalent from the start. In spite of his need and desire, his unconscious mistrust of women, if they failed to live up to his overpowering image, uncorrected by any real experience, of perfect, all-giving, all-embracing mother, kept him suspicious, though he liked me well enough consciously. Unfortunately, before he could let down his defenses against me, there came a dream he simply could not swallow. It showed him in a hopelessly infantile relation to me. He was a babe in the tub, and I was bathing him. That this might be taken as symbolically very positive, he just could not see. Actually, I was somewhat younger than he, and it was too humiliating. He could not face it, so he broke off his analysis. In fact, I think it was probably the only thing he could do. The gap between the dignified judge—and he looked the part, being large, handsome and somewhat portly—and the naked infant in the tub, in the presence of a professional woman who might use his weakness against his already injured ego, this was really too much for one so emotionally crippled.

This man had a gaping void where feeling should be, left by the absence of a mother or any substitute for her in his early development, and he just could not trust me to see his helplessness, as revealed in the dream. I readily agreed to his breaking off the analysis, but tried to keep the situation friendly and maintain human respect, hoping to restore to some extent his self-confidence which had been bashed so badly by the dream. A few years later he was killed stepping off the curb in front of a truck. I could only hope that death, the dark mother, would be kinder to him than life had been. (One of his dreams will be given later about his tragic relationship to his father.)

Much has been said lately about the danger of mothers binding their children to them, and a very real danger it is. But I want to emphasize here also the psychological dangers of motherlessness. By this is not necessarily meant the physical absence of the mother, as in the above case, but the absence of the experience of those life-giving and fostering qualities that is made possible by a suitable carrier of the positive mother archetype. This lack may produce its effects even when the real mother is at hand.

To illustrate this, I will tell you about one of the women mentioned earlier, who had continued to project, at least in one compartment of her psyche, something of the radiance of the image, even though her mother was alcoholic. The father was a professional man, also "a very wonderful person," who, utterly discouraged by the excessive drinking of his wife, just gave up the situation as hopeless. He left his little daughter alone with this woman, not only all day but for quite long periods when he was away on trips connected with his work. During this time the mother was often drunk, and then she would threaten to kill the child if the father were to discover anything about what happened in his absence. The little girl learned how to handle the mother when no one else could manage her at all. But it was by giving her everything she wanted, including complete devotion and constant expressions of it. She had to be constantly flattered and cajoled. The child came to be the mother of the mother, watching her moods and adapting to her wishes.

Of course, she could not do this without suppressing all her own little girl feelings and her overpowering need to be given emotional security by the mother. Instead, she projected her own insecurity upon the mother, whom she saw as a lovely person in the clutches of the devil of drink from which the daughter sought to protect her by an imitation of maternal devotion. In this way her feeling became all mixed up and often extraordinarily unreal. The fact was she had nothing except the mother to stand between her helplessness, the vulnerability of a child, and the frightening outside world. So she had to hold on to any fiction that would enable her to live at all.

The false feeling pattern by which the young girl deceived herself in order to make bearable the bond, and even to exert some control on the adult woman, became fixed as a substitute for true feeling which remained entirely undeveloped and unconscious. So when she grew up, and when feeling was required with her friends, she was a bit gushing, a bit flattering, overadapting to the object in order to take possession of it, as she had done with her mother. But back of this people felt, and recoiled from, the sucking mouth of her shadow—a pitiful starved child, frightened, insecure, greedy with the appetite of a lifetime, but, because of its very insecurity, going over for protection to the false strength of the hostile or paranoid animus, which made her most difficult to get along with.

I should perhaps explain what I mean by the weak, overvulnerable shadow turning to the animus for protection. The shadow may be thought of as the inadequate, insecure, undeveloped and unadapted part of the psyche.[10] The conscious ego should always be aware of,

---

[10] Just as the ego is the subject of the conscious personality, so the shadow is the corresponding figure in the unconscious. Most people try to claim for themselves as many good qualities as possible, with the result that the less agreeable side is repressed into the unconscious where it colors the shadow. The shadow then comes to represent the immature, inferior, auto-erotic and selfish qualities that one prefers to keep out of sight. However, all that is unconscious is not necessarily evil. It may be a value not yet realized in consciousness. So occasionally we meet what may he called the light shadow, a very positive figure foreshadowing the Self. More often in dreams the less acceptable aspect is met, and, because the ego will have

and responsible for, this weaker sister, which is like a child or undeveloped adult, less educated and less cultured. It is a constant thorn in the flesh to the persona, but the mature person carries it willingly, if not gladly, knowing that if it is rejected the powers of the unconscious will either be shut off or will overwhelm the ego.

The woman just described did not at all recognize the hungry demand that showed through when she was saying what she believed were nice and kind things. The shadow had not been made conscious, let alone accepted. Perhaps she dared not realize her weakness, for she did not have a solid enough ego to face it without being swamped. At any rate, she who should have mothered her own child was indifferent to it, and so it had to depend upon the protective attitude of somebody else. But such "somebodies" are not often looking for stray waifs to mother; they expect to be dealing with an adult, and so again the child meets indifference and rejection, this time not from her ego but from the outer world.

The woman's conscious attitude was not hostile or antagonistic to other people to start with, but, failing to make friendly and supporting connections, she naturally was hurt and offended. Having failed to become conscious of the shadow, her ego succumbed to the other figure in the psyche who seemed able to help, the animus.[11] On the surface the animus would seem to be just what is needed, for is not his essential characteristic masculine power, and is this not the necessary counterpart to her conscious feminine personality? But alas, this power animus soon gobbles up unwary little Red Riding Hoods, and then the bared fangs of a wolf are presented to the world. And so an

---

none of it, it naturally joins forces with the animus. See *Two Essays on Analytical Psychology,* CW 7, pp. 65ff, and "The Shadow," *Aion,* CW 9ii, pars. 13ff.

[11] Jung has pointed out that while the sex of an individual influences one's conscious attitude, the unconscious has a contrasexual nature, personified by a person of the opposite sex. This psychological bisexuality is in line with the fact that the psyche is a totality and so contains all opposites, both the dominant and the recessive. The underside of a woman would therefore be personified in a masculine figure (Jung calls it the animus), and the reverse would be true for a man, whose corresponding unconscious figure would be feminine (the anima). These two carry the function of connecting the ego with the collective unconscious. It is because they are unconscious that they are personified or projected, as conscious contents are not. See "The Syzygy: Anima and Animus," *Aion,* CW 9ii, pars. 20ff.

apparently innocent person in whom this has happened would be hard for others to get along with. Quite unconsciously she would demand too much.

I have mentioned the injuries to the child's libido that can come from too much or too little mother love, and how serious the results may be in their lifelong influence. But suppose we have a mother who is as nearly ideal as is likely to happen in a world of imperfect human beings. Would her children be crippled by a mother complex?

Well, I knew the perfect mother once. She was intelligent, good to look upon, exceedingly social and hospitable, and used to hold regular salons in her town house. In summer, her country home was always open to a large circle of interesting people and their friends— writers, artists, men and women of affairs—who came and went at pleasure. She presided over all this with ease and elegance. She never did anything to bind her children to her, except that she was easily the most fascinating and amusing person in their acquaintance. No one of their own age was half so witty or interesting or attractive. They all did marry, but two of the marriages were disastrous, and the third nothing to boast of. I did not analyze any of the family, but a case might be made that this "ideal" mother had an unfortunate effect on the lives of her children.

The mother complex is a universal psychological fact, for it is based upon an archetype which is common to all humanity. I have even seen it amusingly obvious in a dog. No one can escape the necessity to meet and resolve it for oneself. The best mother in the world cannot lift it off the shoulders of her child. The most she can do is to avoid passing on the burden of her own unsolved problems, and to grant her children the freedom and the respect that will permit them to meet their individual assignments independently.

As I have indicated, the mother complex is connected on only one side with the actual mother, however important her role may be. And even when the personal side seems to loom largest, it is the archetype behind that gives it its enduring power. This was vividly expressed in a drawing made by a young woman at the very beginning of her analysis. It was the picture of a human figure, arms extended in the form of a cross, lying as though unconscious or dead on a somber night sea. The figure was enormous, for one could see the arc of the earth which it spanned. She connected the woman with herself.

The patient was an invalid in her early thirties who lived alone with her mother. She told me she had spent the greater part of the last seven years in bed, prey to indigestion, headache, extreme weakness and nervousness. In fact, when she first came to ask about the possibility of analysis she warned me she did not know how often she would be able to keep her appointments, for she could not tell until the same morning whether she would be able to come or not. "Then I can't take you," I replied, with an air of finality. "I cannot hold time for you if you may or may not show up."

She didn't like that one little bit. She thought a moment and then said she would like to try it anyway, to which I agreed. To her amazement, and to my own considerable surprise, she did not miss a single appointment, although she had to come from an awkwardly distant part of the city. Her problem was that she was still inside the mother's womb. The two of them were a typical mother-daughter pair, the one fat and rosy, looking like the cat that ate the canary, the other thin and underdeveloped, like a plucked chicken.

Her drawing expressed the situation perfectly. The night sea is the dark womb of the unconscious, upon which she floats as if dead, in the position of crucifixion upon the mother. She is enormous, filling the whole picture, just as the infant in the womb fills its world. If she can be awakened, I thought, perhaps she may begin to live. This actually happened. She never became strong, but invalidism was a thing of the past. She married very happily and had a son who was a great satisfaction to her. And it all could come to pass because she grabbed with all her strength, indeed with more than she thought she had, the life line that analysis was to her. And soon after the daughter broke free, the mother died . . .

The archetype of the mother is so hard to separate from the real person because, in early childhood, the objective mother is in fact all-important for the physical life of the child and for creating the conditions that allow its psychological processes to get started right. But every step of development reduces her power as an actual person. In the womb, absolutely everything is provided for the infant. It does not have to eat or breathe for itself, and it is protected against the impact of mechanical or thermal stimuli by a water bath of even temperature. But at the moment of birth it must begin to win its independence from the mother. It must learn to breathe, to eat on its own.

Babies vary enormously in their willingness to do this. Some go at it like good little pigs, but others let the nipple slip repeatedly from their mouths, and cry, and altogether indicate quite clearly that they prefer the good old umbilical cord, please. Haven't you seen exactly this in later life?

I recall a woman sent to me by her physician because she was on the verge of a nervous breakdown. She told her story and asked if I could cure her. I replied that I had seen people with her complaint cured, but that it would be a serious undertaking which would take time and the best efforts of both of us. (Incidentally, this approach sorts out those who are capable of being analyzed from those who are not and makes it seem to be a matter of the patient's choice, which is much better than to have me either recommend that they continue or refuse them.)

Well, she thought a moment and then said, "I don't think I need to do this after all, Doctor. I think I would be perfectly all right if some wonderful man was crazy about me." Take the nipple away and give me the cord! I asked her if she thought she could relate to a man in her present condition. But she didn't want to take any responsibility herself. She just thought it would be nice to be carried to some garden of Eden where she would be gloriously raped. "I would be all right, Doctor, if some wonderful man was crazy about me." Then she would not have to go into this business of analysis. Just compare her flaccidity with the strong grip of the patient who drew the picture of herself floating on a midnight sea.

Well, to go on with the process of becoming independent of the mother. First the infant learns to take the nipple, then to give it up for the bottle, then the cup, then the knife and fork—all steps toward taking over functions once performed by the mother. The psychological side of the process follows the same path, but more slowly, and it has much further to go. But it is all overcoming the mother, concrete and symbolic, overcoming dependence upon her. This means taking over responsibility for the fulfillment of one's own needs and the transformation of the libido from passive yearning and needing to adapted action and creativity. It is a tremendous undertaking, for it involves the necessity to find out which needs are real and which must be sacrificed. Consequently the resistance is terrific.

A woman once dreamed that she was masturbating with a fire

fender. This dream actually was the key to her whole problem. Fire is heat, intensity, emotion, violence. It has always been recognized as a god. The fender is what keeps it off, holds it at a distance. Her passionate desire was not to live but to stay at the edge of life, a spectator. Her story corroborated this completely. When she was just under twenty years old, a man somewhat over thirty fell very much in love with her, and pleaded with her to marry him. (Strange, how neurotic women are often attractive to men.) She repeatedly refused. He finally asked if there was not some hope that in the future she might come to return his love. Her answer had been a definite No. A year or so later he died. Immediately she became the heartbroken widow. She made a little shrine in her bedroom where she kept his picture, and on the anniversary of his death her friends would send flowers to lay there. He was the perfect defense against all subsequent lovers. Inevitably she became a veritable "sucking mouth of emptiness." I heard years later, after I had lost all track of her, that she had fallen into a psychotic depression. She had retreated to the womb of the unconscious from which she had never fully emerged.

The regressive mother image seems to offer surcease from struggle, the possibility of easy satisfaction. It is the backward pull to a vanished paradise, the Golden Age of yore, as the myths call it. Whoever would live fully must give all, which demands a workably stabilized center, a certain degree of integration that can hold against the lure of a heart's desire to be had apparently without payment or effort. The mother-bound man never thinks he has to accept life's assignment to stand on his own feet and earn what he wants. And the same is true, of course, for women. "I don't think I will go into this business of analysis, Doctor, I'll just wait for a wonderful man." Inertia or indolence, as La Rochefoucauld has said, is the strongest passion of the soul, more dangerous than any storm. In it is heard the siren song of the mothers, and the terrible mother image presides over the wrecks it produces.

Needless to say, anything capable of producing such devastating effects possesses a power that can be equally beneficent when assimilated. When the mother archetype is experienced consciously as a psychological content, its effects are obvious in both extraverted and introverted aspects of life. As evidenced toward the object, it leads to tenderness, devotion and compassion. There is a nurturing care for the young or the weak and an interest in fostering the development of others, not necessarily children. If this tendency is unconscious or under the control of the animus or anima, it can be a perfect nuisance to the recipient, but from contact with the Great Mother may come the sympathetic understanding of others and the earth wisdom which gives to a conscious individual a light and healing touch.

The symbols of the mother archetype, that is, the images in which she appears in dream or fantasy, myth or legend, are manifold.[12] First, there is the actual mother, grandmother, teacher or, indeed, any woman, usually older but not necessarily so, who gives emotional security or fulfills a need. The concrete reality of the holder of this projection in childhood makes it peculiarly difficult to distinguish the lineaments of the august archetype behind her. Consequently the projection holds the one who makes it to the necessity of living the complementary role, that of a child, long after such an attitude should have been overcome. The unconscious bond occurs in the first place because of an immature psychological condition, which in turn tends to be perpetuated by the reaction of the carrier of the projection. The realization of the symbolic element is the first step toward breaking the bondage to the real person. The next step is the appearance of the archetype, no longer in concrete form but still personified, for instance as a goddess. Demeter, Cybele, Isis, Kwan-Yin, Kali, are such figures, every one of which can also express the negative or terrible side of the Great Mother. There is also the earth mother, Gaia, and in Christianity the celestial mother, Mary.

The functions of the mother, in addition, have produced corresponding symbols for her: fecundity, expressed by the earth itself or a stone representing it, an ear of corn or wheat, the sea, the primordial waters from which all life sprang, matter, which is matrix (mother), the womb and images of it, such as a cave, round hollow objects like a bowl, vase or baptismal font. Other symbols of fertility are the ploughed field, tree, cornucopia, the cow or other animal, the well or spring whose life-giving fluid nourishes all growing things. On the negative side there is the Medusa, the witch or spider, with the meaning of the one who catches and binds the child in her web or

---

[12] [For a detailed consideration, see Sibylle Birkhäuser-Oeri, *The Mother: Archetypal Image in Fairy Tales* (Toronto: Inner City Books, 1988).—Ed.]

with the net of her magic. The mother as the goal of yearning for redemption is represented by Paradise, the Kingdom of God, the Heavenly Jerusalem and many other objects of devotion, such as church, university (Alma Mater), city or country. Death as the womb of unconsciousness and the underworld, as well as Heaven, may have a maternal significance.[13]

Since the mother presides over the feeling and emotional development of the child, she naturally exerts a tremendous influence upon the probability and kind of marriage the child will later make. Indeed, the mother may be quite as important in determining the relation to the opposite sex, even of a daughter, as is the father. A striking and tragic illustration of this was a woman in her early thirties who had been an inmate of a mental hospital for ten years with a diagnosis of schizophrenia. This was her story. Her father had been an imaginative, happy-go-lucky man about town, full of charm and vivacity but quite irresponsible. After leading the mother a terrible life for some years, never faithful but always forgiven, he at last deserted her for someone else. The girl's mother, left to bring up her daughter entirely alone, was naturally resentful and became deeply embittered. She would pour out her complaints of men in general and of the father in particular by the hour. She made her daughter her inseparable companion, engaging all her pity and loyalty, not only against the father, but against all men as exploiters of women, and marriage as the institution for such exploitation.

As she grew up, the girl, though an attractive young woman, had no boy friends and dedicated her life to the profession of nursing. One day she was given the case of a young man who had been seriously injured in an accident. Her sympathy was deeply touched, but she had no idea that her feeling was anything more than this. However, in leaning over the bed to adjust the pillows, her cap "happened" to slip off, and in retrieving it her face came very close to his. She was covered with confusion and hurried from the room. But the next day something similar happened. This time her foot slipped, and for an instant her head lay on the pillow beside him. At that instant the superintendent of nurses came into the room. There was a

---

[13] For additional amplification, see "Psychological Aspects of the Mother Archetype," *Archetypes and the Collective Unconscious,* CW 9i.

terrible fuss about "unprofessional conduct" and so on, with the result that the pride and joy of the younger woman, her nurse's cap, was taken away from her. Soon after, she broke down and had to be sent to the sanitarium.

In spite of having been there uninterruptedly for ten years, she had not deteriorated. She was as neat and dainty as when she had been engaged in her profession. Her speech was coherent and her language good. But she told me that she heard voices all night. I asked her what they said. She answered that they kept making obscene suggestions to her. I asked why she thought they did this. Her reply was one of the most poignant that I have met in all my years of practice. This woman, considered at that time to be hopelessly insane, said something which, if she could only have realized its meaning, would probably have released her from her insanity. She said, with the remote, indifferent little laugh characteristic of her condition, "Oh, I suppose it is to make a woman of me." She wouldn't say any more about it, but giggled a little and lapsed into remoteness.

This woman had indeed been unsexed by the mother, and the unconscious had been trying to make her realize her feelings and instincts as they had been aroused by her male patient. But the resistance was too strong. An irresistible force had met an immovable body. Neither side could give way, nor could the old status quo be restored. So the psyche split into pieces. Even years later in a mental hospital, the unconscious still tried to show her that instinct could not just be amputated, leaving an otherwise intact psyche, but now there was nobody home to receive the message. I could not get her to talk about it again.

Fortunately, the influence of the mother upon the marriage of the child is by no means always sinister. As the exemplar giving the actual experience of eros, the principle of relatedness in the home, it is she who may show the way to flexible and understanding human relationships, and so predispose her children to accept and trust the people they care for, instead of carrying a tinderbox of suspicion ready to flare up at the slightest provocation. A really good relation to the mother is perhaps the best single outer conditioning for a satisfactory marriage.

Now let us turn to a consideration of the father archetype and its effect on relationships. Second only to that of the mother in its fate-fulness for the young, it represents the masculine principle in the home. In traditional families, for tiny children, the father seems rather remote, for he deals with the outside world and matters entirely beyond their small area of consciousness. At that age, even discipline, the application of the father principle of law, is in the hands of the mother, for it concerns adaptation and good habits rather than moral or logical questions. So either the father is a friendly but rather unessential presence who shows up evenings, or be is an aloof figure who inspires fear more than love. Everything really important to the young child is done by the mother, and the father is at best a somewhat awkward assistant. It is still too soon to evaluate the end results in the grown-up children of those modern marriages where the mother also—or instead—has outside work and the father also keeps house.

As the children grow older, the disproportion in the relative importance of the two parents is greatly reduced. In the traditional situation, the mother becomes so familiar in the home that her functions there are often taken for granted, while the father becomes the glamorous figure who goes forth daily into the big world and an unknown and exciting life. The whole household waves him off in the morning and awaits his return in the evening. Usually this is a joyous event, especially if he will spend some time playing with the youngsters when he comes in. There is a feeling that everyone, including the mother, is prepared to adapt to him when he gets home. To the children, this makes him the parent with the greater prestige and authority. The security of the family depends upon the security of his business or professional adaptation, and their social position in the community is chiefly a reflection of his. They boast of him at school and imitate him, as little boys, or try to beguile him, if little girls. But most of all he represents the law within his private world of the home. I do not mean this in the legal sense, but it is his verdict that determines right and wrong, what the children must do and what they must not. This is his role, an archetypal one, of lawgiver, authority, the spirit, as it controls impulse and emotion.

The manner in which the father carries his function of authority is of the utmost importance for the future development of the child. Many people have been seriously warped morally by a father whose rule was based entirely on his own personal wishes and convenience. They felt they were being subjected to a personal tyranny whose only foundation was the fact that he was bigger and stronger. His was the power of the bully, and this violated their sense of independence and justice. The result was that all authority became for them a thing to be evaded or combatted with every ounce of their strength. This is a disastrous blockage of the normal path of development, in which the law of life and of the way things are is gradually discovered to be behind the authority of the father, whose intermediation ceases to be necessary when the child is old and mature enough to deal directly with the inner law. A little boy, when his pals teased him for having been punished by his father, answered stoutly, "Well, I deserved it, didn't I?"

This lad would soon not need the father to tell him whether he had done wrong or not. And the same respect and allegiance he now felt for the verdict of his father would carry over, without too much difficulty, to the laws of outer reality and those of his own being.

On the other hand, I knew another man to whom any "must" was like a red rag to a bull. What Jung calls "the infantile lust for freedom" had not been domesticated or brought into submission to a higher authority. His father had been quite arbitrary in forcing the son to strict obedience, so suppressing the "nuisance," which small boys, to a limited extent, have a right to be, while indulging his own power complex at the expense of the child. This makes the child lawless. But the ego can never be a law unto itself without courting the fate of Phaethon, who drove the chariot of the sun-god, his father, until he crashed to earth.

At first the young must obey the father or mother, then the teacher, then the wise elders of the tribe or society who embody current collective wisdom. This is because the ego is never the whole person and does not know the laws of the totality of which it is a part. Because these laws exist in the unconscious they will inevitably be projected at first, and the most suitable objects upon which to project them are those successive wisdom figures I have just mentioned, from which they may be peeled off when the time is ripe. As the child matures, any carrier of the projection is sure to become less and less satisfactory. The parents become human-sized and fallible. Then rebellion is inevitable. And whether the result will be a new order based on the inner law of integration, or a regression to chaos, will depend to some extent upon the kind of person who had carried the projection.

The father figure, like that of the mother, is frequently neither positive nor negative, or rather both positive and negative, for it is an archetype and so shares its characteristic ambivalence. The father is both loved and hated, feared and revered. A striking case of that sort was a man whose mother had died when he was a small child. The father had devoted his whole life to the upbringing of the boy. The tie between them was fearfully close. They were inseparable companions so the son had very little life of his own suitable to his age and for that reason he also hated his father. They used to spar with each other while swimming, each trying to push the other under. The older man had heretofore been the stronger and could always easily win. But one day in the course of time the youth managed to push the father's head under the water. Without realizing what he was doing, he held it down until he saw that the other was really in trouble and then let him up, half drowned.

The son was overwhelmed at the thought not only that he had nearly killed his father but quite as much that he himself was now a man, actually the stronger of the two. Hence it was the son, rather than his still spluttering parent, who needed help to get to shore. Although he would have been grieved and repentant, and also terribly cut adrift had this relation been severed, nevertheless, something in him would have taken even parricide as a way to freedom.

A more disastrous father problem was expressed in a dream of the judge mentioned earlier, who had been emotionally crippled by the loss of his mother when he was two years old.[14] He too had been brought up alone by a father who was stern and unexpressive. The son looked up to him with considerable awe, but there was very little human contact between them. This relationship also was ambivalent, but with much less companionship than in the previous case. The unconscious fixation, however, is often all the greater when so little of its content can get into consciousness. So the son remained under the father, his libido tied up, yet with very little return from outside. He dreamed:

---

[14] See above, pp. 21-22.

I lived with my father in a beautiful medieval castle, in great comfort and elegance. He had a stable of superb Arab horses, and every year he would challenge all the landowners of the countryside to bring their horses to the castle to race with his. Year after year they came, always with the same result: my father's horses won. Finally there came a year when a span of horses famed for their beauty and swiftness were entered in the contest. Now at last it seemed my father's horses might be about to suffer defeat. The evening before the race, I stood watching as the drawbridge was let down and these magnificent animals pranced into the castle yard, ready for the next day's test. But the possibility that my father's horses might lose was too much for me. I was in panic and felt I couldn't bear it. So in the night I stole out to the stables and put a small dose of some hypnotic into the food of the challenging horses so they would be a little lethargic and thus could not win.

The meaning of this dream is all too obvious. His own masculine selfhood is, of course, the challenger, after the years of submission as a mere boy. The time had arrived for him to overcome the father and take on the responsibility for his own life. He had fine potentialities, as we have seen, represented in the dream by the beautiful horses. The auspices were favorable. But his progressive libido was paralyzed. He could not wholeheartedly even wish to be a man. He was stuck in a provisional life. And, as a consequence, he stooped to fixing the race so he could not win. The early loss of his mother was at least a part of the cause leading to this second defeat.

At first sight it seems incredible that there should be a will to failure in an apparently healthy young person. One might expect that the motive of success would always offer the strongest attraction. But the precarious balance of the opposites in the psyche applies also to the archetypal movements of progression and regression, forward and backward. Peter Pan, the little boy who refused to grow up, is still a familiar figure. The backward pull to regress is commonly expressed by the inability to sacrifice the parental images (not the real parents, as we have seen in the last two cases where the mothers were unknown), and these images continue to rule the unconscious, especially when they have not been adequately experienced in life.

To overcome the father and the mother is to take up the responsibilities of adulthood, to sacrifice provisional living. Then life will surely become harder and more problematic, but potentially more meaningful. It is a momentous step, so much so that primitive peoples, who are close to the unconscious and its eternal laws, celebrate the transition by the always serious and sometimes rather grim rites of initiation. In these ceremonies, performed when the new flood of libido arising from sexual maturation begins to pour into the psyche, the boy is tested for his ability to face pain and danger, and, especially, the fears that come from archetypal sources. If he cannot do this but still needs to be spared and protected, he belongs in the compound with the women and children. If he can take it, his second birth, this time as a man, is celebrated, and he is accepted as one of the young warriors of the tribe.

Now I will relate a dream that embodies a father complex of a very different sort. The dreamer was a woman in her middle forties, gentle, introverted, shy and sensitive. In spite of her self-depreciation, she was highly thought of in the school where she taught and was liked by her small circle of friends. This was her dream:

> I was looking out a window and saw, to my surprise, that the people in the street below were all scattering and dashing about as if terrified. When the place had become deserted I saw a huge black horse, much larger than any in reality, coming slowly down the middle of the street. He was ridden by an enormous man shrouded in black robes. Behind him came a priest, also all in black, carried in a chair by black-robed attendants. Then came three or four black carts filled with black coffins which were empty. Behind this came a black hearse, drawn by black horses with plumes. This too was empty. I was afraid and wondered whom the hearse was for, when my mother, in the most sinister and suggestive way, said, "Take care that the hearse isn't for you."

She was naturally much disturbed by this awesome dream and turned to active imagination to help her find its meaning. The story, in her own words, continues:

> I was looking at my father lying in his coffin as I had seen him after his sudden death. Then I found myself inside the coffin with him. I struggled to climb out, but could not. I struggled and struggled, and all the time seemed to be getting smaller and smaller. I tried desperately to see myself outside, and couldn't.

While telling me this fantasy, the woman bent a paperclip till she had two connected pieces, one in each hand. As she recounted her struggle to get out of the coffin, she was actually struggling to break the paperclip in two. She was quite unaware of what she was doing with such intensity, but the moment she came to the end of the fantasy the paper clip broke and her hands relaxed. I said, "So the separation was made after all?" This was the first intimation the woman had of what she had been doing. She immediately said, "Well, I think I had better tell you another dream."

Before going on with that, let me tell you the material I already had in hand. In the analytic hour preceding the first of these dreams, there had been a rather emotional talk about her relation to her father. The mother had apparently been a domineering tartar in the home and the father had been crushed. The mother despised him. The patient, who felt desperately sorry for her father, never was able to let him know how much she loved and sympathized with him. For this she felt terribly guilty and even partly responsible for his sudden and unexpected death. Thus, the figure who should have been a carrier of the father image, capable of standing firmly between the family and the outer world, and within the home giving wise counsel and just authority, was crippled for the girl. All her vulnerability, all the wounds from the relation to the mother, became identified with his and augmented by them. The authority image, unhumanized by the give and take with a kindly, if also fallible, parent, remained projected onto the outer collective and as a result she was utterly defenseless to every criticism, utterly unable to hold her own.

In that talk she got a fresh realization of her father's fatal weakness and of the life-and-death necessity to overcome the same in herself. This would mean that she would have to take over the responsibility for deciding and defending her own acts, opinions and moral attitudes, without leaning on anyone else. It would seem to be an unmitigated relief to throw off the bondage to the animus of collective opinions. But at least he was *something* to lean on, however uncomfortably, and the patient was still too hurt, between the destructive mother and the weak father, to be able to pay the price of freedom by assuming the responsibility herself. These facts explain the sinister character of the dream.

The dreamer is looking out of the window into the street, which indicates that the action she sees takes place not in her personal psychology but in the collective unconscious. The highly ritualized procession and the dark atmosphere of death show that the dream portrays one of those cosmic and eternal events which are continually recurring in the depths. They are unholy, taboo, and not to be beheld with impunity. Consequently all the people flee, leaving the streets deserted. Realization of such things is, perhaps fortunately, not for everyone. But the depth of this woman's problem forces her to see deeply. All the actors in the pageant that unrolls before her are in black, including the mythologically enormous horse. The climax of the procession is obviously the great black empty hearse. For whom will it be? Her mother, with characteristic heartlessness, suggests it will be for the daughter. But is there another possibility?

I think there is. We have both internal and external evidence that the dream is dealing with the father problem. For the latter, the external side, there is the fact that it followed a moving talk about him, and was in turn followed by the fantasy of the terrible struggle to get out of the coffin with him. Either she would be drawn down to death, sharing his fate, or, if she succeeded in freeing herself, he would go back to the place of shades and she would be released for her own life.

The final bit of external evidence that the hearse may be for the father is the dream I have not yet told. The internal evidence consists of the personnel of the procession. The enormous man on the huge black horse corresponds in size with the father in the eyes of a child, and the priest can be seen as the inner side of the father image. These are surely fit attendants at the funeral rites of the father figure, or alternately of its victim.

The dream then shows that the price of life is a death. It is she or the father. The monumental power of these figures in the dream is the effect of the weakness of the actual father, so the imago is pure, unadulterated archetype. The task for every generation is to overcome the parents. But one rarely finds the heroic struggle so impressively portrayed. It is no mere freeing from a personal parent that is in question here, but the release of a soul to find itself. This is the tremendous drama that lies hidden behind the banal childishness of the family complex.

The fragment of active imagination in which she struggles to get out of the coffin with the father is in the pessimistic tone which is characteristic of her depression. She cannot stand by herself against the strength of the collective father so long as she is crippled by identification with her own unhappy father, whose life had failed in just this realm. But the little entr'acte played simultaneously by her hands, in which the struggle to separate, which she was talking about, was played out with the two parts of the paperclip, reached a successful ending, and the struggle of her hands was released.

Now we can come to the final dream, which came the night following the one just related.

Harriet, a good friend of mine, had killed her father. All her other friends were horrified at this and condemned her for it. But I wondered what dreadful thing had gone before to make her do such a thing.

Harriet was a woman who had been enormously impressed by a man who was a leader in an organization for world peace. She admired him extravagantly. The dreamer recognized a compulsive father element in her friend's admiration. But to throw off all the obligations and demands that were put upon her by family, co-workers and even her friends, and to stand their resentment at her changed attitude was not only a heroic act, but one that produced a feeling of guilt, for all the collective within, as well as without, rose up against her. It is like a parricide and produces a feeling of horror. But in the dream, the patient, recognizing and even sharing the horror of it, can see its inevitability and share also the Promethean "necessary crime" by standing by her friend.

The accomplishment demanded by these dreams is not yet completed by this patient, but they have been important milestones on the way. They illustrate in an extraordinary manner the powerful effect of a weak father in shaping the problem of a son or daughter, but it must never be forgotten that what the individual does with the problem is his or her own business. Everyone's life in childhood is conditioned, in a way that is quite beyond one's control, by the particular parents and by environmental circumstances. But when as adults we blame somebody else for what we are, we thereby give evidence that we are still in the psychological cradle and have not yet taken moral responsibility for our own acts and attitudes. To the wise, circumstances and people are the raw material out of which to make a life, giving stimuli or warning, encouragement or temptation to despair, but always the chance to experience and, in the process, to crystallize a Self. In pursuing our individuality we replace blind Fate with meaning and choice.

The realization that adulthood involves a tremendous overcoming of childish dependence and the control of impulse is painfully missing in our civilization. Growing up means to many young people the right to demand more privileges and pleasures, more freedom from parental authority and supervision, with no corresponding assumption of responsibility. They expect to be allowed to drive the family car to drinking parties, and to return at whatever speed they can get away with. This kind of freedom is their idea of adulthood, and if father or mother is so stuffy as to put up any objection, they complain they are being stifled.

I was talking some time ago to a young fellow, a senior at college, who came to see me because he had lost all incentive. His marks had fallen off to such an extent that he was worried lest he should not be allowed to graduate. He had never been a particularly good student, but the previous year he had done well and for the first time had an excellent record. He said he did this just to prove to himself that he could, so his difficulty was not lack of brains but of motive. Now he no longer saw any reason for hard work. It simply had no meaning for him. The boys in his group, a fairly well-to-do lot, could see no sense in trying to get high marks unless one aimed to be a "greasy grind." Serious work became something a little less than manly. They saw no value in this opportunity to prepare themselves for their future life work, either to acquire important facts or techniques, or to learn how to use the mind. And above all there was no idea that they should now be tempering the steel of their own psychological instruments, acquiring the discipline to be able to sacrifice immediate pleasure for a more distant goal and a meaningful life.

I did not attempt to analyze the young man. He had to get back to college so we had only a couple of hours together. Anyway, I doubt whether analysis of the unconscious would have been desirable for him yet. So we just talked about these things and I asked him a lot of questions that made him think, he said, as he never had done before. The upshot was that he returned to college and graduated satisfactorily. The fact that, at the time, all healthy college boys were expecting to be called up for service in the Korean War immediately after completing their studies tended to drive them either toward overseriousness or toward a frivolous attitude in the intervening time. If you are going to get killed soon anyway, what's the use of studying now? You may never get any return for it, so you might as well get all the fun you can while it is still possible. So, the parents pay the bills and the grown-up son, figuratively speaking, sucks the bottle. If our civilization had initiation rituals equal in dignity to those of primitive tribes, there might not be such a waste of the time and morale of our young men. But, of course, such rituals cannot be made up artificially. It is the psychology of the collective community that has produced the attitude of these boys and allowed the importance of symbolic performances to vanish.

Incidentally, I should tell you a little about the father of the student we have been talking about. What was missing in his life that might possibly have given enough realization of inner values to have saved his son from falling into such a slough of autoerotism and meaninglessness? The father was an extraverted thinker whose socially adapted ego was one hundred per cent involved in work. He was a professor of economics and sociology, and, in addition to his academic work, he had undertaken an enormous amount of social improvement activity. From this, rather than from his teaching responsibilities, he received his greatest satisfaction and sense of accomplishment. He was a man of great uprightness, but not much imagination or psychological insight. Other than his solid dependability and his enormous capacity for hard work, which amounted at times almost to a compulsion, he had little of the inner life to share with his son, who had a great respect for his father but no wish to follow in a similar pattern for himself.

So the boy's drifting was in part an unconscious protest against the kind of rigid law embodied in his father's life. Instead of betting on his own horses and carving out a new and more congenial way for himself, he was brought to a standstill; he would not go his father's way yet he was too bound to him and to the mother image of easy satisfaction to create his own. Fortunately he was young and might still wake up and do something effective about it.

You see from these cases that though the mother archetype is the dominant one for little children, later on that of the father is quite as fateful. For boys it carries the strength and authority they need to fulfill their ambitions and it connects them with reality, mind and the spirit.[15] The wealth of meanings contained in the father imago is shown by the variety of symbols under which it appears. His activity and power may be expressed by the horse, the bull, the hero, thunder; his authority by the ruler, the state, the law, police; his fertilizing power by rain, rivers, the phallus; his wisdom by the wise old man, the light bringer, the logos; and his spiritual quality by wind, lightning and, finally, by God. These aspects of the meaning of the father image merge and the same symbol may express several of them at once, as, for example, the bull, which may represent physical power as well as fertility, and so on. They add up to images of the creative principle at all levels.

When the father archetype is assimilated it gives clarity and strength; it enables boundaries to be set; it gives an inner source of authority which is no longer the ego but comes from the old wise man speaking for the Self. It is the measurer and leads to understanding. Through it the character solidifies. Creativity begins to flow and there is the will power needed to work along with it. And finally the place of the father is taken by the image of God.

The parents influence the children almost as much indirectly by the kind of relationship between them as by that with the child. Of course, in human experience nothing exists isolated and in pure form, but is inextricably mixed up with a multiplicity of other elements. Father, mother and the relationship between them cannot be clearly differentiated in their effects upon the family. For example, the previous illustration of a fatal mother identification in the girl who became a nurse and later a psychotic could equally well have been described from the point of view of the conflict caused by the attractive but irresponsible father, or by the split between the parents as reflected in the vulnerable soul of the daughter. Such overlapping of causes is the rule rather than the exception. Not only does the kind of marriage the parents have create the atmosphere in which the child lives, but the daily example of the way they relate to each other tends to be reproduced later in the life of the child. If this atmosphere is one of good will and harmony based on well worked out problems,

---

[15] See "Mind and Earth," *Civilization in Transition,* CW 10, pars. 65-66.

it leaves a faith that love and mutual understanding are possible in a home, and a certain degree of experience of how they may be fostered. Where there is constant bickering and resentment, these are assumed to be the inevitable way that one must defend oneself with other people. Meanwhile, the ill will and hostility in the environment continually rub the child the wrong way and keep it in a state of bad temper. When it goes to school, it easily comes to be regarded as a "problem child."

The ego is very frail and unformed in the early years. It exists in a state of unconscious oneness with the unconscious of the parents and so is utterly vulnerable to any poison in their psychology. If the parents can handle their side of the problem, the child is free to deal with its own, which is the inevitable enterprise of growing up. Otherwise one is apt to remain stuck in helpless and regressive reactions to the adult emotional situation, where no adequate orientation or understanding is possible. For parents who love their children, this danger constitutes a strong incentive to put their own house in order. More will be said about this in the chapter on marriage.

So far I have spoken of family relationships chiefly from the point of view of the son and daughter, and the effects on them of the parents and parental archetypes. Now I want to turn to the point of view of the parents and what they experience through the child. The birth of the first child activates in them those important archetypes of father and mother we have been discussing. The parents do not generally think of themselves in that capacity until the confrontation with their own baby lays upon them the necessity to enact the new and strange half of the child-parent combination. All the enriching possibilities of the mother and father archetypes have been lying fallow in the unconscious, waiting for this experience to stir them into active being. The child and parent, especially the mother, are one unit in the unconscious, where a complete identification prevails, only a little less fateful for the parents than it is for the child. Their loving tenderness is strongly touched and all life becomes more serious because they have given a hostage to fate. A young married man of my acquaintance used to differentiate between couples in his circle who were "brat conscious" and those who were not. He and his wife, because they had a little family, preferred to flock with experienced and knowing parents.

But again the important experience of parenthood is not just that of the real babe, for all its appealing charm and helplessness. There is also the archetype behind it. The child is the possibility of eternal life in this world (for the parent). But also the unknown possibilities in this new little life make it a carrier for the image of the Divine Child, the newborn Self, which symbolizes the rebirth and individuation of the parents. This is one reason why it is so awfully hard for them to allow the child any deviation from their ideas of how they would like their own next chance to work out. The poor little thing often has its life all cut out for it before it is fairly out of the cradle. A friend of mine, a recent widow, told me in all seriousness that her boy of four was going into the diplomatic service to become an ambassador. Quite frequently a mother, dissatisfied with her marriage, instead of trying to do something about that will cherish a fantasy of her daughter's redeeming her personal failure by making a marriage after her, the mother's, own heart. Of course, the very clinging to the daughter that this unconscious claim indicates alienates the daughter and prompts her to try to evade every effort to bind her, unless she happens to have a strong counterprojection. Such a mother is hard to escape, for she seems on the surface to be not the man-eating shark she is in reality, but a pitifully unhappy parent, asking only for a little love from her child.

I have seen women who grew up in an atmosphere like this. Their whole emotional life went underground and became half-consciously evasive, inarticulate and inadmissible even to themselves—all as an unrealized escape mechanism from this kind of mother. Unable to hold their own against the pull of her libido, their deeper feelings dropped into the unconscious and so became unreachable. It is inevitable that the more the older woman wants to live again in the younger, the worse will be the relation between them and the less the satisfaction either one will derive from it.

It is never safe to have one's entire adaptation and sense of security tied up in the relation to a single person, but when that person is one's child it is absolutely fatal. For the child *must* escape. From this point of view, the relation of the mother to her child is apt to involve great suffering. In the beginning the identification is necessarily close, and the care of the child so much a part of the woman's metier during its infancy and early life that a tremendous bond grows up, especially if the husband is dead or the marriage is unhappy. It demands an almost superhuman sacrifice to accept the law of nature and let the emotional center of the young life pass on to someone else. But if a woman lets herself become nothing but mother and has no other important relationships or occupations, she comes to have no other way of functioning, and even if her own children make a getaway—no mean feat—she goes right on mothering everyone in sight, thereby becoming a perfect nuisance. "Did you take your umbrella?" "Have you got your rubbers on?" "Don't forget to take your vitamins."

I remember once walking along a fairly high precipice with a friend and two young men, her son, a man of twenty-nine, and a contemporary acquaintance of his. They were both able professional men, entirely capable of taking care of themselves. But the mother began clucking, "Don't go so near the edge," "Be careful," "Watch your step," and in less than no time she had both men scrambling up and down the bare face of the cliff in a really risky way. It seemed to be the only way they had to get free from mother's apron strings.

You see, to grow up psychologically it is absolutely necessary to find one's own boundaries, to choose actions from a unique personal center rather than parrot someone else or echo collective opinion. Any decent education will take this into account and allow the young person to experiment up to the limit of real danger. If the right or safe way is always dictated in advance, one does not come to any personal judgment. Anyone who is not a complete ninny will experiment anyway, but in doing so one's attention will not be fully given to making the right judgment, the one that really fits the situation, but will be caught in irritation at being always told what to do. This emotional intrusion clouds mental functioning and may have serious consequences. As Jung once remarked, there is many a boy in prison just for committing an act he was sure was his own because nobody else would approve of it, an act that was really a passionate declaration of independence.

For either father or mother, the only hope of retaining the friendship of their adult children is to let them go their own way. However difficult it may be to see someone dearly loved making what look like terrible mistakes, the right to make them must be recognized. The son or daughter who has come of age should be treated with the respect and noninterference granted to anyone else. He or she has a right, and a most important one it is, too, to make whatever mistakes are necessary in order to find their own path.

Of course, this hands-off policy toward grown sons and daughters is, at least partly, predicated upon their actual attainment of autonomy. When they expect to be supported and to have their enterprises bankrolled by the family, they have not earned their freedom. I remember a contemporary of mine in medical school who recognized and accepted this limitation on her freedom. She would have liked to smoke as the rest of her colleagues did, but her parents were most strongly opposed to it. In those days, women outside the professions had not generally accepted cigarette smoking. My friend refrained entirely until the day she graduated and was on her own financially. She said that as long as her father was supporting her through medical school, she felt she had no right to do what he objected to, unless it involved her personal obligations or individual morality.

But there is another side to this. What about the parents' duty to remain independent? If the children should earn their independence, should not the parents also? Obviously this does not apply to those cases where an act of God such as illness or age has incapacitated one or the other, making a willingness of the strong one to help a matter of common humanity. But suppose one parent dies and the children are married or otherwise fully occupied. Should one of them necessarily make room for the relict?

Well, I will make no generalizations but will tell a story illustrating one such situation and what happened.

It is the case of a man whose wife died when he was seventy years old and about to retire from business. He had been a devoted husband and it was feared lest he go to pieces at the loss of so much all at once. People wondered which of his two grown daughters could possibly make a home for him. But he announced that he was going to stay on in his apartment with his excellent housekeeper to take care of him, that they needn't worry about him at all, though he would be delighted to see them anytime. There was no pressure and no pitifulness on his part. The result was that they loved to visit him. More than that, their friends did too, and, whether expected or not, they would often drop in. It was heart-warming to be met by his welcoming smile, to hear him call out to the housekeeper to ransack the icebox and bring out its best. In this way he made real and devoted friends of his children. Someone once teasingly asked him whether he would rather have an old-fashioned daughter or a friend. "But," she added, "if you choose the filial daughter, you must never ask if she really means it when she makes an affectionate remark!" He answered with conviction, "I am very content as it is."

So even between parents and grown children, as in any other combination of adults, the relation is better when both sides preserve what independence is possible, and, where help is required, that it be given or received not as a right but as a mark of affection. The way many daughters and sons recklessly throw away their own lives in taking care of a parent may be a noble devotion in their own eyes, but actually is no less a complex than the case of the mother who "lives for" her children, and it is no more likely to increase the actual good will between them. There can be more weakness than altruism in the woman who cannot do anything that would make mother think she was an ungrateful daughter. Each situation should be met on its own merits. There is no universal rule that one should be grateful to one's mother. It is no favor to the child to be brought into the world. This happens as a fulfillment of the lives of the parents, who then owe it a chance for a decent amount of health and happiness. I once read of a man who sued his son to recover the cost of his education. The court wisely disallowed it, saying that in becoming a parent one assumes the responsibility to use the ordinary means to fit the child for the station to which it was born.

Motherhood is no more sacred than any other relationship, indeed is not sacred at all except for the experiences that may, and usually do, go with it. Where the great archetype of mother has been carried to the best of a woman's ability, it usually leaves a sense of deep appreciation in the child, but this bank account of good will may be overdrawn. How much is left will be one factor in determining how much the son or daughter can give the mother when the tables are turned and the older woman is in need of material assistance or human contact. Yet love is not a bargain, it depends entirely on the other fellow's deserts, and the more one can give, the more richly one lives. So it is apparent how inadequate are any generalizations about what is owed to an elderly parent—how much is an obligation one would not feel right in shirking, and how much is a claim from which one must struggle mightily to be free.

I will give an illustration of a conflict of this kind in a woman who fortunately had had quite a lot of analysis. Her mother had cancer, which had reached the stage where, though she was not entirely bedridden, she was confined to the house and actually lying down most of the day. But she needed attention sometimes four or five times in the night. She did not think that actual nursing was required, and, being very introverted, she hated to have a stranger in the home. She naturally preferred to have a member of the family do for her. She and her husband and a maid were the only ones in the apartment, so all this care fell mainly upon him. He was a business man, no longer young, and the strain was simply too much for him. So she asked her daughter, who was a teacher holding a responsible position and living at the other end of town, to spend the nights at home and be on call.

The daughter realized she could not do this without the risk of breaking down; yet the situation of the old people was tragic and touched her deeply. So she said, "I cannot agree to what you ask as long as the need is due to your refusal to have a nurse. If father will do it, that is his decision. If you are willing to let me get a nurse for you, I will stand behind whatever necessity arises. If the nurse leaves or is unsatisfactory, then I will gladly fill in, to any extent necessary. But otherwise I am sorry but I can't do it."

At first the mother still rejected any alternative and the father carried on alone. But soon the patient herself realized it was too much for him and gave in. This case was a terribly difficult problem for the daughter because of her deep sympathy with the father as well as with the sick mother. She saw that he was reaching the breaking point, but she also realized that it would do no good for her to get there too, when all that would be accomplished by it would be a few days' or weeks' delay in making an obviously necessary move. It is hard to put any discipline upon one who is already mortally ill, but, as a practicing physician as well as an analyst, I am convinced it is no kindness to encourage or abet the loss of morale while there is a spark of consciousness left.

There is a test that is very useful in helping someone, perhaps a daughter, as in this case, to find the way between compassion and self-defense. It is this: Is the one who is sick or in trouble willing to

submit to her own need and to sacrifice her privileges and prefer-
ences in adaptation to it as far as possible, or is she demanding that
the other person make up to her for her misfortune beyond the point
of necessity?

I have seen a man, for instance, so neurotic as to have no boundaries at all, absolutely refuse psychological help, yet require his wife
to be the slave of his every caprice to save him from panics or
tantrums. She had to carry the unbearable weight of his neurosis
until, at the breaking point, she was forced to cut loose entirely. Had
she had the strength and discipline herself, she would have insisted
that he submit to the necessities of his condition first, and allow her
to help as far as she was able where he really needed it, which she
would gladly have done. In this way the final break might have been
averted, and with it a vast amount of resentment on both sides.

Another case concerned a dominating mother who was completely
paralyzed and bedridden for nineteen years. During that period, or
within a few years after, her husband and no less than three daughters committed suicide. If she could have given up her rule of the
house from her bed, perhaps her daughters could have made something of their own lives. But they were perpetually torn between
compassion and resentment. Their primary identification with the
family unit had never been challenged. Death seemed to be the only
way to individual freedom. Even within a family, especially of
adults, each individual has his or her own separate fate. Misfortune
certainly strikes through one to another, but the relation of the two to
the blow is, and should be, different. The one upon whom it falls
has the stark necessity to adapt to it, but the others have some degree
of freedom, either to offer what love prompts or to serve what they
accept as their obligation. But there is no right of one to climb on the
back of another.

I heard about this ingrown family from the paralyzed matriarch's
granddaughter, who finally broke the family curse by taking it to
analysis. The problem was beautifully expressed by a dream which
showed the way in which outside relationships were distorted by the
overwhelming family bond. In the dream the granddaughter was returning after a short absence to a house she owned jointly with a
woman friend who was with her. There they found in possession an
uncle and aunt, who had dug up many of the plants on the place and

were putting in others which, according to their own opinion, would be nicer for their niece, the dreamer. The friend, who very much preferred the original plants, protested, but the dreamer shut her up, saying she must not hurt the feelings of the uncle who thought he was doing them a favor. There the dream ended.

At first she couldn't see the point when I said the friend was perfectly right. The house was owned in common and neither one should allow her family to take liberties with property only half of which belonged to her. "But," she protested, "I did not want to hurt my uncle's feelings!" It was hard for her to realize that, if the alternative was passively to permit him to encroach, not only on her life, but on her friend's too, his feelings would simply have to be hurt until he learned to stay on his own preserves. "Good fences make good neighbors," says the old skinflint in a poem of Robert Frost. But I should rather put the words into the mouth of the wise man. Boundaries, psychologically as well as geographically, should be violated only with consent and good will. Indeed, in this case the amount of pain the girl would have to cause would depend to a very great extent upon the way in which she spoke to the uncle about the situation. I shall have more to say about this matter of boundaries in the chapter on friendship.

Before leaving the subject of severing the tie between mother and child, it is interesting to consider what is done about it in India. For this purpose I will quote from the description of a Hindu ritual called The Giving Away of the Fruit. Its object is to break the mother's fixation upon her son.

> This is a ritual which the spiritual guide and life-long housepriest of the family (the "Guru") enacts with the mother of the household while her son is growing up. This ceremony is a kind of weaning away of the mother's soul from the overpowering possessiveness of her love for her male child. . . . In a symbolic procedure, accompanied by tales, the Guru acts out the relentless demand made by life and the outer world upon the mother, to surrender her dearest treasure, to give him up to the world and to his own life-career, a demand that can only be fulfilled by sacrifice.[16]

---

[16] Henry R. Zimmer, *"The Guidance of the Soul in Hinduism,"* in *Spring 1942* (The Analytical Psychology Club of New York), pp. 43-44.

Accordingly the mother has to offer to the Guru a long series of objects, beginning with the fruit she likes best, which the Guru proceeds to eat in her presence while she fasts. Later he asks her for some metal object, at first an inexpensive trinket, then more and more expensive ones, then gold, until she has given him a substantial part of her jewelry, which, outside of her clothes, is about the only exclusively personal possession of the Hindu woman.

> This ceremony is repeated during several years, and is marked by a definite gradation. Through it the mother is trained . . . to surrender what she cherishes most. She grows mature enough to face the final sacrifice toward which these offerings, gradually increasing, are meant to lead her. The Guru watches her attitude. When he ascertains that she is ready to face the supreme sacrifice of giving away the dearest fruit of her life, the sequence of offerings reaches its climax.
>
> The final ceremony is enacted before a solemn assembly. The male relatives and representatives of various castes and professions are invited. These symbolize society, professional life and the world at large, which the boy is about to enter. The assembly of males represents the order of the adult, the future sphere of the youth, to which the mother is asked to surrender him. Society, the world, life, accept the sacrifice of the son from the mother; they witness his departure from her lap, and from her dominating influence. . . .
>
> On this occasion the mother, who rules the household, offers a feast to the whole company, while she herself fasts; and throughout the whole day she is not allowed to sip even a drop of water, a peculiarly trying observance in the Indian climate.[17]

The parents who have been able to refrain from holding onto their children and left them free to go their own way may then be granted the inner experience of the Divine Child, which represents the birth of Selfhood within the psyche.[18] The divine, or hero, child is one of the most important archetypes in the family picture, and it is always a great sacrifice to avoid concretizing it. In terms of the Kundalini process of development, the step through the diaphragm to the Anahata chakra is the hardest of all, for here it is that Ishvara, the Lord or Self, is first glimpsed. The lure of the outer world is tremendous, for

---

[17] Ibid., p. 44.
[18] See "The Psychology of the Child Archetype," *The Archetypes and the Collective Unconscious,* CW 9i.

it is the colorful veil of Maya and holds all of reality in the early part of life. Many people turn away from taking the next step to the inner achievement, even some who have started on an analysis.

For example, a woman who was having serious trouble in her marriage realized that she herself was the cause, chiefly as a result of her own psychology, and that she had a long way to go before she would be capable of a workable relationship with her husband. She thought she would attempt it anyway, but it was no surprise to me when she announced a short time later that she had decided to have a physical baby instead. She stopped using contraceptives and promptly became pregnant. Her libido was quite naturally caught up in this, and her analysis, equally naturally, came to an end. But so did her marriage. From my knowledge of her husband it was evident all along that she would have to overcome her autoerotism if she were to have any chance of holding him. She thought, as many women do, that a flesh-and-blood child would do the trick of tying him to her, and it would be a great deal easier for her than a serious analytic endeavor. So the upshot left her angry and disappointed. Her fate would be to struggle along in Maya for many years more, if indeed she would ever transcend the stage where the world and what she wanted of it was all she could care about.

Dreams containing the symbol of the birth of a baby often come when the patient thinks the problem is only to find the solution to some outer difficulty. They point to the psychological truth that solutions of any major problem do not come from the head. What is required is a renewal of the entire attitude. The impasse plunges the patient into apparently hopeless conflict. But out of the struggle may come a dream of transcendence of the opposites in the form of the birth of the hero child. None of the major conflicts of life are soluble, but it is just when the tension becomes unbearable that rebirth can happen. But only if, in the language of the alchemists, the retort is kept closed and the mounting libido is not allowed to leak out and be dissipated in external things. This kind of continence was impossible for the woman just mentioned. Her libido did leak out, and so she bore a physical, not a spiritual, baby. She remained bound to the Wheel of Fate, which turns and turns but does not change.

There are other patterns of relationship that should be included in the family category, though they are much less fraught with destiny.

Chief of these is the relation between brothers and sisters. Though this does not usually touch such depths as do the others we have discussed, it plays a considerable role in the formation of friendships, which will be taken up later. Also sibling rivalry and identification may be a very important factor influencing development. Adlerian psychologists consider it the most prolific cause of neuroses, at least in children. Values, even traits of character, may be parceled out in the family, this to one, that to the other. And no one is supposed to encroach on the territory of another. This is particularly apt to occur when they are of the same sex. If they are girls, one will be socially adroit, the other bookish, or one will be serious and the other flighty. They thus complement each other and may become fast friends, but jealousy may erupt and set them at each other's throats. Similarly with boys, one will be mechanical, the other intellectual, one dominating, the other gentle and artistic, and so on. On the whole, comradeship flourishes best between individuals who are, to a considerable extent, alike in age, sex, tastes, common interests and temperament. But the consequent danger of identification is always immediate. All this will be more fully taken up in the chapter on friendship.

Other family archetypes are the stepmother, popularly pictured as a negative mother, the grandparents, who are the somewhat magnified and depersonalized parents, and the godparents, in whom the depersonalization has gone much further and the suggestion of the divinity of the archetype has been added.

This is only a rough sketch of the family archetypes which exert such a formative influence upon subsequent relationships. Their influence differs in character from that of any other archetype, for they are part of the original world of unconsciousness into which the child is born. There is not yet any awareness of, or objectivity toward, anything. The child simply swims around in the primordial soup and is part of it. The basis of this whole world is the mother, and, later, both parents. When a little spark of consciousness does begin to appear, it affects only the top layers, leaving the original state of identity untouched. In addition, the actual people who first hold the projection of the family archetypes are in themselves a matter of life and death to the child. This reality is so fundamental and is so completely taken for granted that it requires a great deal of psychological sophistication to see them as "mere symbols."

The primordial identity with the family, a state in which there is no individual consciousness at all, is terribly hard to break. Often it is never accomplished. That is why family members rarely treat each other with the courtesy and consideration they would unhesitatingly give to a stranger. The feeling seems to be: "My close relative is just a part of me, so I do not have to show consideration for his feelings as a separate person. I can say what I think of him unasked and expect he will not be offended." Either there are no secrets at all—everything is spilled out naively and as a matter of course—or everything of real concern is strictly hidden, as an unconscious reaction against dissolution of the family.

The letters home of college students, for instance, are apt to be one long burble about the interesting things going on, behind which the writers remain quite invisible, with no word about any real or deep reaction to it all. I have often seen middle-aged sons and daughters, married and professional people, who make their visits "home," as they still significantly call the house of the parents, and yet they offer only their dead bodies, like zombies, for the parents to enjoy if they can. They share only externals, and it is with relief, frequently on both sides, that when a suitable time has passed they get up to go. The gap in age between the two generations is naturally part of the barrier. But adults often have friends with whom there is no difficulty in bridging an even greater difference in years. The real cause of the strangely rigid and unreal element in the family situation is that each side still projects the archetype onto the other. It is still a case of the collective roles of mom and dad and the kids rather than a real individual relation.

Younger people hesitate to share their experiments with life, their successes and failures, except superficially, lest their parents interfere by worrying unduly or giving heavy-handed advice, or gobble up the still unassimilated experience in order to show off their children to their acquaintances. The parents, on the other hand, dare not reveal their weaknesses or inner conflicts, which become more oppressive with advancing years, for fear that they will lose their prestige, and anyway "the children would never understand." So this sad isolation of people who might really be dear to each other goes on, often till death. The frustration it produces leads to irritation when in each other's presence and dries up all feeling. Haven't we all found that the last place where we could feel or act like an adult was in the presence of father and mother?

The answer is not geographical separation, though this may be necessary as a temporary expedient in the process of getting free. But I have seen plenty of people whose parental complexes have merely remained unconscious instead of being assimilated, though they have lived away from home for many years. Put them back with father and mother if you want to see how free they really are. Maturity that depends on geography or any other external condition is highly questionable. One can't run away from oneself. And it is pretty hard on parents to be avoided simply because they have become scapegoats for the immaturity of their children. I do not mean that it is necessarily desirable for the generations to stay near by, but it certainly is not desirable either for them to have to run away to escape the realization of their childishness.

It is often difficult to know whether the persistence of a family fixation is due to the inability of the parents to let go or to the clinging of the younger generation. In either case an exaggerated bond between them will usually produce bitter resentment and strife. But nothing is too strange to happen. I have seen such a fixation taken for granted as ordinary Christian kindness in the home, and work like a miracle.

Let me illustrate this contrast by two examples. Some years ago a friend and I stopped at a farm run by a woman with three grown daughters, all of whom had jobs in the near-by small town. On Saturday one of the daughters came home saying she had been invited to spend the next weekend on a motor trip to Albany, a city some distance away. Motor trips in those days were not as common in the country as they are now, but without giving reasons or doing anything to soften the blow the mother gave this classic reply: "No, my dear, your Albany is by your mother's side." One could not mistake the smoldering anger and sense of frustration in the daughter.

The opposite situation, where the fixation seems to all concerned to be the result of a healthy family relationship, was demonstrated by a former college friend of mine. She was a professional woman who in middle life acquired an automobile. This was years ago, and in those days cars were not regarded as a universal necessity but as a rather special treasure. She told me she was happy as a clam exploring the country. The next time I met her, I asked about her new toy. She answered quite calmly and as a matter of course, "Oh, I don't have it any more. It made father nervous to have me on the road, so I sold it." Just like that! No protest, no resentment; not even a sense of any particular virtue. One just didn't make father nervous, whether reasonably or not, and there was nothing more to it.

This was so incredible that I could not have believed it was more than a facade if I had not known her pretty well. She was not a meek person; yet her individuality allowed her to live according to her family's Christian mores, without the slightest friction. She so fitted the pattern that it did not kill her libido. She did all the conventional things as though they were her own idea and she had never had to struggle to adapt to them. And the strange thing is that the pattern contented her right up to the day of her death in her early sixties. The family was just one part of a collective culture that fitted her like a glove. She lived and died with less conflict than almost anyone I have ever known. In spite of being a concrete-minded, factual person, she remained in Paradise before the Fall right to the end. And incidentally she had lots of friends who regarded her as a wonderful person.

The powerful archetypes of family relationship lend the power of unconscious forces to ordinary life and their assimilation brings the possibility of the radiant or uncanny quality of the gods into the realm of human experience. But they also may blight instead of intensify. Which is it to be?

It seems that the effect, whether they bring blessing or curse, depends upon how the individual relates to them. When the mother image is constellated in a young woman with her first baby, it raises her to a level transcending her past experience. She is filled with an overflowing devotion of great power and beauty. It is the natural counterpart of the helplessness and mysterious potentialities of the babe. That this emotion is not from her personal psychology but comes to her from the collective depths makes it none the less her experience and her opportunity to be changed by it. If this happens in her, she will not have to hang on to the child to make it constantly renew this maternal satisfaction for her. But if nothing happens within from the experience of motherhood to leave a residue of the wisdom of the heart, of tenderness and compassion and humanity, then she is likely to push the child away as soon as possible and return coldbloodedly to her personal interests, or keep it tied to her when it should be gaining its independence, or else go on having babies in order to renew the feeling of fulfillment.

When the activated archetype is the true pattern in the unconscious for the existent life situation, and when a conscious relation to it has been gained, the result is a deepening, an intensification and a greatly expanded meaningfulness of the whole experience. In this case it will be possible later for part of the libido inherent in the maternal archetype to go to the inner process, and so release the rest to pass on, as love and devotion, to the real child as a separate personality. Such a transformation in the libido of the parent allows the intensity to be retained without trying to force the child to remain static as symbol holder. But when the mother's feeling clings to the child after infancy, the warmth gradually goes out of the relation for she is only going through the motions of object love; she is cold to the actual child except insofar as she can make it enact her unconscious image for her. The love is stuck within her own autoerotic circle; it does not get beyond herself and what she wants. I have often said that this kind of love is like that for rare roast beef. There is not much the beef will get from it.

The mother is the beginning and end of the journey of the soul. At first she is the security and warmth in which it can grow, then she becomes the temptress who lures it to turn back from life, held by the ease of childish dependence from developing its full potentialities in the great experiment of life. Then it is driven from her by the necessity for self-realization, or else by the lash of a symbolic incest prohibition; but after long wanderings, it finally returns to its roots and unites with the mother, this time as a symbol within. The full cycle is completed, the start in the unconscious, the eviction from Paradise, the extraverted adventure in the world with, perhaps, the hero's deed, and at last the introversion for Self-realization and what Jung has called "the last great achievement of death."

This, then, is a brief sketch of some of the meanings of the universal experience of the family archetypes.

2

Men and Women

When first the infant, with its little spark of consciousness, opens its eyes upon the world, the archetypal and habitual relations of the people around it are already in full swing and make up the pattern of the way things are. Now we turn to a relation that does not begin until somewhat after the time of puberty, namely that between men and women.

I want first to refer to Jung's two contributions of extreme importance to the subject of male-female relationships. The first is his idea that the masculine principle is expressed by logos and the feminine by eros.[19] The second contribution is his idea of the animus and anima.[20]

Before the work of Jung, the discussion of relationship between the sexes suffered from the lack of any practical differentiation of what was to be considered masculine and what feminine, as soon as one passed beyond the biological sphere where all was perfectly apparent. Ideas on the subject differed widely. There are many traits and activities treated as belonging to one sex in one civilization and to the opposite in another. Once smoking cigarettes was thought to be unbecoming in a woman. Then there was a time when some young men said they didn't smoke because it was regarded as too effeminate. The Chinese have parallel concepts, yang and yin, but they are rather more cosmic than specifically psychological.[21]

---

[19] Logos, in Jung's terminology, is the creative understanding which he takes to be the basic psychological characteristic of the masculine principle. The feminine counterpart of this is eros, the principle of relatedness, whether the relation be to people, things, ideas or circumstances.

[20] See above, note 11.

[21] In Chinese philosophy, yang and yin are opposed and complementary principles. Yang is the principle of Heaven. It is bright, warm, strong, active, masculine, creative. Yin is the principle of Earth. It is dark cold, moist, receptive, feminine, fecund and nourishing. They are basic principles governing the universe, including human psychology. From the tension between them, as from the poles of a battery, comes the energy of both the organic and inorganic realms.

58

Into this confusion Jung brought the underlying principles of eros and logos, which, though intuitive rather than scientific concepts, furnish a touchstone from the psychological angle and bring the possibility of order into chaos. Naturally, as is usually the case with great new discoveries, others have realized something like it before. Swedenborg, for instance, said that man represented the love of truth, and woman the truth of love. But with Jung's clearer differentiation, it becomes possible to see how man and woman are mutually complementary, psychologically as well as physiologically. It is the way the sexes complement each other that is of the greatest interest to psychology, for it is responsible by far for the largest part of the emotional drama that plays eternally around their relationship.

As the psyche contains both the opposites, while consciousness is dominated by one or the other, the hidden part will be of the opposite sex and will be personified, as unconscious contents tend to be, appearing in dreams as the soul images which Jung has called the animus in a woman and the anima in a man. These numinous figures, because unconscious, will usually be projected onto the opposite sex. If this does not happen, they do not cease to be effective but will contaminate the ego and produce one of those undifferentiated types—a mannish, animus woman or a womanish, anima man.

Thus, in the man-woman relationship, each party stands facing the other in the objective world, but with the archetype, animus or anima, just behind his or her shoulder. And, as this inner factor is not usually recognized as playing a part in the situation, its explosive power consequently seems to belong entirely to the other person, who thereby gains a compelling quality, as though somehow casting a spell. But the magical fascination is in fact the effect of the unconscious soul with its vivifying and potentially completing power. Because the deepest longing of the human being is ultimately for wholeness, the unconscious other side will exert a tremendous attraction upon the conscious personality. When it is recognized that these figures represent one's very soul, without which one feels empty, incomplete, devoid of meaning or value, it is not surprising that their projection may give rise to the most violent passions, and that the loss or faithlessness of the object onto whom they have been projected may indeed seem to be a fate worse than death. It is no joke to have someone else walk off with one's soul.

The masculine mentality is predominantly impersonal, analytical and discriminating. It tends toward investigation and formulation and is likely to cut a man off from the earth and warm human connections; but the woman onto whom he projects his anima can give him a sense of rootedness in the earth and of all the color, vitality and magnetic allurement of life, without which his mind is cold, solitary and forbidding. Two examples from very different sources will illustrate this. The first shows a glimmer of the masculine-feminine differentiation even in tiny puppies just beginning to run around on the rug and take an interest in the world in which they were such recent arrivals. These were three little Sealyhams, one male and two female. The male was an explorative little person, extremely interested in everything he could discover, tireless in his researches concerning the nature of his world. He was perfectly good tempered, but, all said and done, people were not the important thing in his eyes. His two little sisters would disport themselves happily enough on the rug, but if anyone approached they almost invariably would leave their play and run over to be petted and cosseted. They obviously took a greater interest in relationships.

The other example is a thumbnail play written by a little girl for her English class. It is so short and so pat that I can't refrain from quoting it in full.

Act I. Place, the camp of the continental army in the American revolution.

First revolutionary soldier: "Gee, ain't it awful this revolution ain't got no flag!" Second revolutionary soldier: "Gee, ain't it awful!"

CURTAIN

Act 2. Place, the same.

Second revolutionary soldier to George Washington: "Gee ain't it awful this revolution ain't got no flag!"

George Washington: "Gee, ain't it awful!"

CURTAIN

Act 3. Place, living room of Betsy Ross's house.

George Washington, "Gee, ain't it awful this revolution ain't got no flag!"

Betsy Ross, "Gee, ain't it awful! You hold the baby while I go make one!"

FINAL CURTAIN

The down-to-earth quality of the woman could hardly be better expressed.

Men are apt to be quite dependent on their women in meeting a social situation. It is not anything the woman actually does that he needs, but her mere presence seems to connect him with his anima and thereby enable him to function well, perhaps, indeed, even better than the woman. This was evident in the case of a man with two grown daughters whose wife had died. He was a most friendly, feeling extravert, and, very important on the practical side, had an excellent housekeeper, entirely capable of managing the arrangements for any entertaining he might want to do. But he never cared to give a dinner party, even a small one, unless one of his daughters could be present. They did not know his friends very well, nor was the combination always a very congenial one. But with one of them at hand, the man could be a most delightful host.

Woman finds the realities of human contact her natural bailiwick.[22] It is the sky rather than the earth that is opened to her by the projected animus, revealing significance and impersonal truth behind the events of life and relativizing her personal concerns. The mind of a woman is usually first awakened by a man, but it need not be one with whom she has a close or intimate relation. The intellectual or spiritual animus often has the impersonality referred to in connection with the masculine principle, logos. He may be a teacher, a preacher, a commentator or a writer from whom she has received no personal attention at all. In spite of that she may imagine she is in love with him, for anything so vital to her can stir her eros reactions.The man is more apt to need a sexual relation with the carrier of his anima, because she embodies human warmth and feeling and emotion. The projected anima enables the man to bring his feelings, and therefore himself, into actual life. To the woman, traditionally limited to an attitude of mere responsiveness, and dependent upon the leadership of a man for direction, the animus may give freedom, through the ability to know her goal and to pursue it consciously. It also gives the

---

[22] See "Woman in Europe," *Civilization in Transition,* CW 10.

courage, initiative and perseverance to hold out in spite of opposition. The anima gives man the earth connection and an inner sensitivity; the animus gives woman a general truth and the principle of order. Between them, they represent psychic forces arising from the unconscious—in the one case leading to the feeling and emotional side of life, in the other to that of mind and spirit.

Of course all this is tremendously generalized. There is the spiritual anima also, as embodied in the Virgin Mary, Sophia, Beatrice, as well as certain goddesses. For feeling has its spiritual aspect, and, when the lure of Maya is overcome or perhaps frustrated, the libido turns to the inner world where it meets the inspiration of the spiritual anima who may also have been prefigured in a projection onto a real woman. And for the overintellectual woman, the animus appears frequently as a man of physical strength and down-to-earth knowledge, like a gardener, a carpenter or a sea captain. But in both these cases, the man with the spiritual anima and the woman with the earth animus, there will generally be found a holder of the more usual form of soul figure. The same woman may be both earth and heaven to a man, or he may worship the Virgin and find a very different sort of recreation with a more sensuous partner. A woman often can love the simple, earthy kind of man and at the same time be stimulated mentally by an animus projection onto a writer or an inspiring speaker. The concepts we have been talking about must never be taken as dogmatic theories with which to pigeonhole the infinite varieties of human experience, but rather as tools to help in understanding it.

The anima and animus soul figures are not only archetypal, they also have a quite personal side capable of great diversity as colored by the particular life story. The anima is strongly conditioned by a man's mother, either by similarity or contrast, as well as by the social and feeling values of the community in which he grew up. Moreover, she is apt to embody the psychological function most remote from the one he consciously adapts by.[23] If he is an intuitive

---

23 [Jung's theory of typology identifies two personality attitudes—introversion and extraversion—and four basic functions: sensation, thinking, feeling and intuition. In brief, *sensation* tells us that a thing exists; *thinking* tells us how it works; *feeling* tells us what it's worth to us; and *intuition* tells us what we can do with it. See Daryl Sharp, *Personality Types: Jung's Model of Typology* (Toronto: Inner City Books, 1987).—Ed.]

type, the anima will be especially earthy, perhaps even coarse or obscene. But if sensation is his major function, the anima will plague him with all sorts of hunches, often negative or actually misleading but occasionally very profound. The animus, in a similar way, is influenced by a woman's early experience with men, beginning with the father. Here the effect is chiefly apparent in the realm of ideas rather than feeling. In spite of the individual differences in their origin and how they manifest, there are enough common elements to make these two figures recognizable as perhaps the most powerful archetypes controlling the destiny of the adult human being. And since the factors which are unconsciously active in the psyche are invariably projected, it is small wonder that the man and woman to whom this has happened have such symbolic, as well as practical, importance for each other. They are held together by a bond which can be broken only at the cost of losing a sense of life, indeed, losing the soul itself.

We have seen that the man-woman relation is really not just a twosome but a foursome, with two of its components human and two archetypal.[24] Now I want to say a few words about what a dominating daemonic animus or anima looks like in life, for the unconscious partners must never be forgotten or they will take control from behind the scenes. A most dramatic illustration of the projection of an evil animus was given in *Trilby*, a novel by Daphne du Maurier. When Trilby was a very young girl, her animus was caught by Svengali, a terrible man with hypnotic power, who, having discovered that she had a magnificent voice, exploited her almost somnambulistic docility for his own sinister purposes. She was as helpless as a bird in the power of the evil eye of a serpent. She became a famous singer with an immense success, but without Svengali she could not sing a note. He used her, broke her and threw her away. The hypnotic power which enabled him to do this depended on the projection of her animus. She had a great natural gift and should have taken the responsibility for it herself. Instead she was only yin, a passive female; the power heaped up in the unconscious till it had to be projected and thus she was trapped by the mad Svengali.

---

[24] See "The Psychology of the Transference," The *Practice of Psychotherapy*, CW 16, pars. 421ff.

Anyone who projects these figures of the unconscious falls under their power from outside. But *not* to project them, without having made them conscious, leads to no better an outcome. When this happens, the ego becomes identified with them and so gets all mixed up with the animus or anima. In marriage, a woman of this kind will, as the saying goes, wear the pants, and such a man will be tied to his wife's apron strings, as he had been to his mother's. The animus of the woman will either make her become the husband of his anima, which, incredibly, sometimes even seems to work for a time and after a fashion; or else her animus will make her fight him day and night as though she were another man. In the latter case, if he can keep himself right side up and not get caught by his anima, he will figuratively, if not literally, beat his wife up a time or two, or have the good sense to leave her. If the fight goes on and on, it is because his anima has joined in—he meets the woman's aggressive animus with passive resentment and then bitterness. No one can say that such a marriage works for anything but the forces of hell.

The goal of being able to relate simultaneously to the partner on the outside, and to the animus or anima within, is the peculiar challenge to this generation. We are forced to go to the psychological roots because of the collapse in a large portion of the population of the effectiveness of the religious and social forms, which, as Jung has shown, were once able to contain and express the unconscious.[25] But few moderns rely on the idea of the sacredness of marriage or a candle lit at a holy shrine to carry them over a serious difficulty in a relationship. Either they are caught and held on the horns of the dilemma, or they have to scratch around for the psychological insight which can enable them to surmount the problem.

The chief responsibility for taking the lead in problems of relatedness naturally falls upon women, for their governing principle of eros makes them more at home in this sphere. It has been my experience, for instance, that, when a marriage is on the rocks, if the wife comes to me for analysis there is frequently a good chance of saving the situation, but if the husband alone comes there is not so much hope, even when he is the one chiefly at fault.

Take, for instance, a man who realized his excessive drinking was

---

[25] See "Psychology and Religion," *Psychology and Religion,* CW 11.

alienating his wife and turned to analysis. He found the roots of his problem in himself all right, and tried to reform. But it didn't work. The patience of his wife, who demanded results, wore thinner and thinner. Because of her unhappiness and reluctance to get a divorce, she decided to come for analysis too (separately, of course). Only then did things begin to improve, due to a change in her attitude. Rather than being friendly and open to a restored relatedness, she had actually been remote and critical, waiting for the father image to be carried "properly" by her poor husband. She thought he should give her the kind of relation she longed for, without her taking any creative part in making it possible. Alter some analysis she ceased her immature demands; she risked investing her feeling in the situation before it was guaranteed to be secure, and so made a bridge by which he was able to cross over to her. She became able to carry the eros role, without which the man could neither reach her nor change himself.

Though women are so deeply concerned with relationships, it is an interesting fact that the precarious state of modern marriage has been almost deliberately precipitated by them, for feminists have smashed the old forms and assumptions which protected it as an institution having the full backing of men. This is particularly strange because marriage was probably in the first place a concession to women on the part of men. On the biological side, the sex act for the male is an urgently required release of tension, involving no entangling consequences. As his pleasure is enhanced by the youth and novelty of the object, it is easy for him to become a gay Lothario. But for a woman, it is altogether different. The sex act may leave her pregnant, facing the pain and possible danger of childbirth, and after that she has to look forward to years of time-consuming obligation to the child, amounting almost to a career. This is too much for her to cope with alone, so she has had to learn to hold herself a little aloof, to be a bit coy and hard to get, until the man is thoroughly committed and ready to sacrifice his freedom to gain the woman of his choice.

These characteristic attitudes of the male and female of the biological *genus homo* correspond, either as cause or effect or however you like to regard it, with the more psychological differences in the way men and women view the erotic relation. Men seek a vivid, poignant or ecstatic experience, which they take, according to the stage of their inner development, simply as an acutely pleasurable gratification or as a moment of intense fulfillment in which the powers of the body find their apotheosis. Men want this experience, need it, and are driven to it by life itself. This is not the main thing for a woman. She wants love, understanding and a depth of communion that make for a unique personal relationship. She is not seeking a particular experience of the moment, but a particular man with whom she may have a lifelong union. Usually it is the man who makes her realize the possibilities of sexuality in cementing and renewing a relationship. And, in turn, the woman shows him that a far greater depth and satisfaction are possible, even in the sex act, when it is an expression of love as well as desire. Indeed, after the stage of blind passion is over, their sexual reactions to each other often become a sort of barometer, indicating the state of their feeling relationship. Actual impotence in the man and a complete lack of response in the woman may have no other cause than that their rapport has been disturbed.

So each opens a new realm to the other, yet not quite new either, for each has longed for a lover to make come true the strange yet familiar vision of the animus or anima. But this secret image usually fails to be understood as a psychological content or to be assimilated by the conscious mind. In that case, the characteristic tendency of each sex, inadequately compensated by the opposite principle within, is to exploit and dominate the other for its own purposes. The man will try to use the woman for his pleasure, while the woman will want to tie the man up for life before giving him anything. When he wants to take her to bed, she asks, "Do you love me?" and he replies, "How on earth would I know until we've made love?"

The biological tendency that leads women to seek a permanent basis for relationship in the form of marriage emphasizes the paradoxical fact mentioned above—that they have been the ones to tear it down. "Away with the double standard!" cried the champions of women's rights. If men were to be free, so they would be too. They rushed to make themselves independent of men socially, intellectually and economically, and to compete in gainful occupations. Some even went so far as to ape the clothing and manners of men, unaware that they were proving their equality by abjectly undervaluing everything that belonged to them as women, going over to the masculine side completely.

This unlovely phase has been rather more than adequately casti-gated, I think, by women who now sit in complacent possession of the values for which the feminists sacrificed so much. For the whole turmoil among women, beginning with the suffragettes and the ad-vocates of women's rights, represented the upsurge of a new spirit in them. Apparently it was necessary to destroy the old forms and re-strictions which had expressed the life of the past in order to clear the decks for a fresh start. Woman's acceptance of the idea that her place was, under all circumstances, in the home, even that of someone else, was replaced by a desire, even a compulsion, to escape from the home and to force a way into every traditionally male occupation. She had to find her limits for herself, who she was and where she organically belonged.

But this attitude of vigorous, often violent, pushing, thrusting, dominating and ever restlessly experimenting with life is, of course, diametrically opposed to the feminine principle of yin and due largely to the emergence of the masculine animus. For all its rationalizing and intellectualizing, it indicates a movement in the unconscious of women, strong enough to suspend temporarily their inborn feminine attitude and to make them rivals, sometimes even envious haters, of men, capable of throwing away their greatest traditional security, the sanctity of marriage. They wanted more than a safe form and they would take no substitute. I suggested this was done deliberately, but now we detect the forcing hand of the animus on an enormous scale, making women of a whole generation pawns in a cultural change springing from the Zeitgeist, which they could not at the time fully understand. This movement from the unconscious was apparently almost suicidal to the individual, but it was so widespread that it seemed to boil up from the depths of the collective, irresistibly carry-ing all in its way before it.

The early adherents of a new movement are often really its vic-tims. They may live and die without knowing whither they are being carried, or what, if anything, their sacrifice will bring about—for themselves or for others. But perhaps it is not too wild a surmise to see in the struggle for a woman's right to find herself in the outer world the precursor and preparation for a similar quest on the psy-chological level. The fact that such a large proportion of Jung's early students were women may be attributed, I think, to an attempt at the individual assimilation of the spirit that first erupted collectively in the early feminists.

It is too soon even now to try to say what is the central meaning of that feminine unrest, but we begin to get some perspective on it. The very nature of yin makes it possible for a woman to become merely the feminine counterpart of a man, a syzygy, like one of the tiny female figures held in eternal cohabitation in the lap of an oriental god. Her impulses readily make her adapt, adjust, fit in, for she projects her law, her formative power, her overall view of life, onto the man, and by conforming she feels completed, at least from the outside. Yin is verbally inarticulate, not contentious, closer to a state of nature than yang, and so a woman finds it harder, however much she may talk, to defend herself in words that are clear and cogent and meaningful to the man. For this she would need both the ability to analyze her feelings and a central relation to the Self. She can hardly come to this while she remains under the shadow of father or husband. She has to stand alone, unsupported by men, sometimes even against them. Hence the replacement of feeling in militant feminists by an ugly power psychology.

Of course, without some sense of personal power the woman can hardly hold her own against traditional conventions in which the place and functions of her sex are all predetermined. But her real task is to discover who she is in herself and how she can proceed further from her own roots. It is all the harder to do this convincingly when the value she is defending is only dimly conscious and still contaminated by all kinds of rationalizations. The animus has to take the lead in the outer world to champion a spirit not yet completely clear. Unfortunately, all too often this has resulted in methods that are exaggerated, compulsive and lacking in consideration for others.

In our time, the woman who was completely identified with her biological role opposite man has had to meet the disturbing impact of her sister who denied him any importance at all in her life; and when she was caught by instinct, which never tamely submits to theory, she has tried to handle the situation as a man would, that is, by an assumption of complete freedom in her sex life. This has led her to poach on the time-honored preserves of the wife, so ending some of the comfortable stagnation of marriage. The woman who has caught her man can no longer drop into a taken-for-granted security, but has to be on her toes lest the lone wolf steal him away.

Well, the women of today have learned the value of freedom, not only for their individual development but also for the fullest experience of love. One of the most widespread archetypes of femininity is the virgin goddess of the earth or the moon. Virgin does not here mean to be without sexual experience. These goddesses were quite the contrary. Remember Artemis, Aphrodite, Persephone. Virgin in this sense means "one in herself," that is, whole, free, not existing solely as the anima of the god. Olive Schreiner, a distinguished South African writer, published before the turn of the century a little book called *Dreams*. I will quote one of them:

> I saw a woman sleeping. In her sleep she dreamt Life stood before her and held in each hand a gift—in the one, Love, in the other, Freedom. And she said to the woman, "Choose!"

This was the dilemma of nineteenth-century woman; so indeed in the dream she is torn with anguish.

> And the woman waited long, and she said, "Freedom!" And Life said, "Thou hast well chosen. If thou hadst said Love, I would have given thee that thou did'st ask for; and I would have gone from thee, and returned to thee no more. Now the day will come when I shall return. In that day I shall bear both gifts in one hand."
> I heard the woman laugh in her sleep.[26]

That dream expresses in a nutshell the basic truth of eros.

Ralph Waldo Emerson has said, "The condition which high friendship demands is the ability to do without it." The same thing applies to love. If we cannot do without the friend or lover, it means either that we have been using the other to satisfy our own wishes, or else to stuff up a hole in our mandala. Neither belongs to relatedness. Woman is learning that, in relating to her man, she must also keep in touch with a strong, independent, upstanding animus in herself, so that she may dare to face squarely and accept the inner truth of the situation, whether it should lead to a deeper togetherness or to a breakup of everything. For this reason it is also important that the woman achieve, or already possess, a degree of financial independence, so that she shall not be helplessly tied to the man by the ne-

---

[26] Olive Scheiner, *Dreams* (London: T. Fisher Unwin, Ltd., 1890), p. 79.

cessities of the breadbasket, but can take the risks inevitably involved in working through the difficulties of a conscious mutual adaptation. Serious problems and divergences of view must necessarily occur from time to time when the lives of two separate adults are closely joined. In relationships that begin in extreme youth, the personalities are more malleable and are readily molded to fit the shape, each of the other. But in later life the personality has crystallized and individual circumstances and responsibilities have assumed an obligatory character. Then the problems of adjusting to a new partner are considerable, even with the greatest good will. Only a real inner independence can save the woman's yielding from becoming abject, and her adaptation to her partner from being a falsification of herself.

In a truly magnificent study of Amor and Psyche,[27] Erich Neumann goes right to the heart of the problem in relationship, which, he realizes, is for the partners to find each other as individuals. The myth itself is a gem, expressing the anonymous approach of the masculine partner to sexuality, which is taken by Neumann as a nonpersonal ecstasis, a "paradise in the dark," as he calls it, a momentary union of two strangers, with no touch of human relatedness in it. This corresponds with what we have been saying about the eros of the man. He experiences it through the anima, so it has the transcendent, superhuman or subhuman quality of the unconscious, the realm of instinct and the archetypes. It may have a terrific poignancy, passion, sublimity even, but it is too far from his consciousness for him to be really in it. It just happens to him, without his being aware either of the meaning of the experience to himself or of the individuality of his partner. The real person behind the anima projection remains as much "the unknown woman" as ever, and the depths, if plumbed at all, are plumbed without his conscious participation.

Indeed, a man's conscious attitude may even be extraordinarily childish and inadequate. He may treat coitus as though it were no more than the king of indoor sports. Or it is the ultimate mystery of life, which he may drink quite impersonally from the woman. And all this is because, unless he has an unusually good relation with his anima, the realm of eros is simply out of his range of vision, so he

---

[27] *Amor and Psyche: The Psychic Development of the Feminine* (Bollingen Series LIV), New York: Pantheon, 1956.

prefers to let it go automatically, and not have to accept it in the open where it may be talked about. It is certainly desirable that the evil eye of a managing or prurient consciousness should not be turned upon it, nor should it be touched at all without a good rapport and as a sincere attempt to release the flow of life from some perhaps unnecessary obstruction. But eros is the realm where a woman lives, and she may be able to enter it by daylight, and so find the way for the man as well as herself to drink more deeply of the waters of life. She knows, in her being if not in her head, that the Moon Goddess (to use the symbol that Esther Harding has chosen to express the erotic aspect of the eros principle)[28] has her own peculiar laws, based on the way things are, and hence how you must act if you are to go with, instead of against, the life current. This is the "must" of the mother, as distinct from the "ought" or "should" of the father. It is the potentiality given in nature and the natural course of growth. The woman is closer to this, even if she does not understand it. Her very femininity *is* eros. And here the man, with his discriminating principle of logos, is handicapped. His dissecting, analytic, differentiating mind sets him over against nature, which he tries to dominate and control by his scientific method and logical thought.

Some readers may be disturbed at what may seem to be dogmatic generalizations about men and women that do not take account of the infinite range of human variation. You will think of men who have been the most wonderful, tender and considerate lovers, with a capacity for great depth and devotion, and, on the contrary, of women who have a perfect genius for irritating and inflaming past endurance the sore spots of their partners. What of them?

Two chief factors account for this, without invalidating the general rule. The first is the fact that the totality of the psyche contains all opposites. If one characterizes the conscious mind, the other will operate in the unconscious. And since the anima of the man plays a leading role in the field of relationships, her quality and the nature of his relation to her are most important here. Another factor determining the kind of relation a man will make is his past experience of women. If his mother, for instance, was wise as well as devoted, so

---

[28] M. Esther Harding, *Woman's Mysteries: Ancient and Modern* (New York: Pantheon, 1955), pp. 48-63.

that his connection with her was strongly positive, he is likely to have an openness toward other women. But if his relation to his mother was bad, he will have no friendly anima to mediate, and so no connection with eros, or worse, a purely negative one. And in the case of the woman, the animus, as we have seen, may overlay her femininity until she seems to have no natural connection with the Moon Goddess at all, only a ready-made opinion to meet every situation. This too is influenced by the father and other men in early life.

But to return to Neumann's commentary on the myth of Amor and Psyche, every word of which brings to life meanings in the relation of woman herself, as well as of the anima of the man, to the eros principle. I will quote a few passages. As you will see, Neumann comes to exactly the same conclusions that have been forced upon me by years of analytic practice and life experience.

In the myth, Psyche, against the express command of her unknown lover Eros that they were to be together only in the darkness of the night, lights a lamp in order to discover who he really is and finds that he is the god. She had felt compelled to see him so that she could know and relate to him. Neumann writes:

> We must not forget [that] Eros himself did *not* want such a Psyche! He threatened her, he fervently implored her to remain in the paradise-darkness, he warned her that she would lose him forever by her act. The unconscious tendency toward consciousness (here toward consciousness in the love relationship) was stronger in Psyche than everything else, even than her love for Eros—or so, at least, the masculine Eros would have said. But wrongly so, for though the Psyche of the paradisaical state was subservient to Eros, though she had yielded to him in the darkness, she had not loved him. Something in her, which may be designated negatively as matriarchal aggression, or positively as a tendency toward consciousness and a fulfillment precisely of her feminine nature, drove her imperiously to emerge from the darkness. It is in the light of knowledge, her knowledge of Eros, that she begins to love.[29]

It was the drop of flaming oil dripping from Psyche's lamp which in the myth awakened Amor and caused him to depart.

The oil as essence of the plant world, an essence of the earth . . . is

---

[29] *Amor and Psyche,* pp. 80f.

significant as the basis of light, and to give light it must kindle and burn. Similarly in psychic life, it is the heat, the fire of passion, the flame and ardor of emotion that provide the basis of illumination, that is, of an illumined consciousness, which rises from the combustion of the fundamental substance and enhances it.[30]

In her horror at having nearly killed her divine lover, Psyche accidentally wounds herself with an arrow belonging to him.

Psyche wounds herself and wounds Eros, and through their related wounds their original, unconscious bond is dissolved. But it is this two-fold wounding that first gives rise to love, whose striving it is to reunite what has been separated; it is this wounding that creates the possibility of an encounter, the prerequisite for love between two individuals.[31]

This means that every relation deep enough to stir the unconscious involves a preliminary merging of the two personalities, in an identification, with mutual projections and loss of old boundaries, which are to be widened in the experience. If the identification is prematurely or rudely broken, the cement holding the two people is torn out, and they are then apt to fly apart due to the libido that formerly held them together turning negative. But if they can stand the pain of the wound caused by breaking the identification between them, then the "being in love" that brought them a sense of their original unity may be transformed into real love.

The myth continues with Psyche, desperate at the departure of her lover, setting out to find him. She asks help from the great goddesses in vain, until Aphrodite, mother of Eros, who is terribly jealous of the girl, promises success if she is able to perform a series of impossible tasks, each one so dangerous that it will almost certainly prove fatal. However, various kindly spirits warn Psyche and tell her how to avoid the risks and attain her end. But, after fulfilling the last task, she disobeys the goddess and as a result falls into a deathlike trance. When Eros learns of this, he rushes back and awakens her. There is a reunion of the lovers, but this time in the full light of consciousness and shared love.

---

30 Ibid., p. 84.
31 Ibid., pp. 85f.

Thus we see that a love which begins as passionate desire, may, for spiritually sensitive people, be but the first act of a drama whose beginning is on the level of nature, where the human being is caught in forces that threaten to overwhelm. But sooner or later circumstances arise, often produced unintentionally by oneself, in which this passionate libido has to be sacrificed. This is tantamount to a death, as in the trance of Psyche. But the death may lead to rebirth, in which the libido becomes no longer a blind force of nature, of which the individual is really an unwitting victim, but the expression also of a transcendent choice, in which the conscious will and the nonpersonal forces are reconciled. Such an experience is felt to be deeply religious, though no theology may be involved.

Of this Neumann writes:

> With Psyche, then, there appears a new love principle, in which the encounter between feminine and masculine is revealed as the basis of individuation. From the standpoint of Aphrodite as a nature principle, the union of feminine with masculine is not essentially different in man and in the animals, from the snakes and wolves to the doves. But once the relation between Psyche and Eros has transcended this stage through Psyche's act, it represents a psychology of encounter; a uniquely loving one fulfills his existence through this love, which embraces suffering and separation.
>
> For the first time Psyche's individual love rises up in mythological rebellion against the collective principle of sensual drunkenness represented by Aphrodite.[32]

Finally Neumann turns from the development of the two persons through the man-woman relationship to the symbolic level, where it becomes a universal inner drama of the soul's relation to God.

> For two millenniums the mystery phenomenon of love has occupied the center of psychic development and of culture, art, and religion. The mysticism of the medieval nuns, the courtly love of the troubadours, Dante's love for Beatrice, Faust's Eternal Feminine— all reflect this never-resting mystery-like development of the psyche in woman and man. It has brought both good and evil, but in any event it has been an essential ferment of the psychic and spiritual life of the West down to the present day.

---

[32] Ibid., pp. 90f.

This love of Psyche for her divine lover is a central motif in the love mysticism of all times, and Psyche's failure, her final self-abandonment, and the god who approaches as a savior at this very moment correspond exactly to the highest phase of mystical ecstasy, in which the soul commends itself to the godhead.[33]

And here is one last passage to indicate the place of the mysteries of Eros which may be experienced through a fully realized love.

While the masculine mysteries start from the priority of the spirit and look upon the reality of the phenomenal world and of matter as the creation of the spirit, the feminine mysteries start from the priority of the phenomenal, "material" world, from which the spiritual is "born." In this sense the patriarchal mysteries are upper and heavenly, while those of the feminine seem lower and chthonian. . . . The two are complementary, and it is only taken together that they yield an approach to the whole truth of the mystery.[34]

Now after this excursion to the top of a mountain from which we had a sweeping view of the heights and depths, the meaning and potentialities of this business of men and women, let us come down again to sea level and the consideration of some of the details visible only from the plain. Let us take another look at modern woman.

As a result of her relatively new emphasis on the individualistic side of her nature, woman has lost contact with the archetypal feminine in herself. This should be her conscious principle, as her grandmother knew instinctively, and it seems ironic that she should have to learn it again at all. Yet it is a common experience that those things which have been lived unconsciously since the beginning of time may have to die as automatic or natural responses, in order to be reborn as conscious knowledge and voluntary action. One does not go directly, as by a straight line, from purely natural automatisms to conscious control in that same area. On the contrary, the spiral movement goes over to the opposite side of its round and comes back on a new level. It was so with Psyche, who could not change from the stage of the "paradise-in-the-dark" to a conscious and redeemed love. Instead, she had to lose love entirely and work on her own. Then, when she herself was transformed, so also was her

33 Ibid., p. 140.
34 Ibid., p. 149.

love. And so also it has been with modern women. They have had to learn to think independently, which, of course, is the only kind of real thinking there is. And for that they had to free themselves from identification with men, which, for a while, involved the sacrifice of love. But when the tool of thinking is made conscious, it can be used in the service of eros instead of against it. This subject will be dealt with further in the discussion of conscious relatedness.

But, while the typical modern woman needs to reconnect with nature on a more conscious level, there are still plenty of the old-fashioned ones who have never extricated so much as a little finger from the archetypal matrix of yin. For many women even today, the relation to this collective core of themselves is one of total identity. They are unaware of themselves as in any way differentiated from it. I have had such patients and they are just like water. You try to get them to stand up for themselves in the open, or to put themselves consciously on record, and they simply can't do it; it is just unimaginable to them. They may quietly and bafflingly bring to pass what they want, without ever expressing it openly or connecting it with the wishes or objections of the other person involved. They are essentially indirect in their methods and always seem to be pulling invisible wires.

If they knew what they were doing, I would have no objection, but often their course of action is not intentional at all, appearing as a spontaneous manifestation of that serpentine path Jung speaks of as so characteristic of natural movement. Their constant desire seems to be to get, and hold, the approval and liking of the person they are with. They are naturals as anima carriers. But sometimes the wish shows through the soft exterior—to get and keep possession of the coveted object, be it inanimate or human. These are the flowerlike girls who so often turn into middle-aged termagants when the underside comes to the surface. But superficially, it appears instinctive with them to want to please, to attract, and to be sought after. Frequently, but not always, such women spend a large proportion of their money and time on clothes and do all they can to make themselves as alluring as possible, quite unaware that sooner or later they will surely send a bill for their overadaptation to the man. I have heard one of them even hotly deny that there was any motive at all back of the make-up and perfume, and she thought it insufferably nasty (which it probably was, though true) when a man coldbloodedly asked her, "Why do you put out the honey if you don't want to attract the bees?"

Once I had a patient who reacted as anima, not just of one or two men, but of any man she met, as unconsciously as an automaton. Naturally she thought men were interested in nothing but sex. Soon after she came to analysis, she dreamed:

> 1) I was on a stage, doing a kind of striptease act. Then the dream suddenly changed, and I was in the midst of a crowd of men who were doing a violent sword dance. I was not adequately clothed, but I could not escape, and was pierced painfully through the arm.
>
> 2) I was again on a stage, and was singing as I never thought I could.

The striptease act is an absolutely promiscuous appeal to the instinct of the men. She was consciously the polar opposite of the sort of woman one might expect to give such a performance. She had been brought up carefully in an oversheltered home, was tremendously tied to her mother and just a bit frightened of men. But she was also a healthy little animal, and, not being able to relate to them otherwise, she jumped compulsively into the anima role. She did this not only sexually, for she was charming and, though infantile emotionally, was in many ways intelligent and had on occasion even been a *femme inspiratrice* to various musicians and artists. But as long as she promiscuously appeals to men by her unconscious femininity, they will appear to her as dangerous phallus bearers, as they do in this sword dance, and she cannot escape being hurt.

It is an anonymous member of the crowd who penetrates her with his sword, and the stab wound is not in her heart or her genitals, as we might expect, but in the arm. This strikes her effectiveness, in a certain sense her power, for what she gets is never what she really wants, which is love. It is actually more real power in herself, more ego development, that this woman needs in order to hold her own with men. She does not know how to protect herself from their unwanted advances, consequently she feels bruised and injured by them. She is really not of the harlot type, so the wound is painful. Compare the dream of a woman who was closer to that type and who had had many men. She dreamed her vagina was outside her body, like a little sac, where she could have intercourse without being emotionally touched or in the least disturbed by it.

The second fragment of the dream given above showed the effect of even a small amount of analysis. She was singing beautifully, as she had never dreamed she could. This suggests that if she can express her true feelings she will not have nearly so much to fear from men.

Fortunately, the undiluted anima attitude went pretty much out of style in the suffragette generation, principally because it smacked too much of heated subservience to men, but also because it was in conflict with the exaggeratedly meticulous honesty, animus inspired, which refused to use any wiles or artificial means to attract. "I want to be loved just for myself," these women said, all too often meaning for the limited little conscious personality.

But now a few women, no longer blind to the archetypal reverberations in human relationships, are learning to use from the right motives means which they had rejected before because the motives were frequently ambiguous, if not positively reprehensible. The desire to attract comes from the basic feminine principle personified by the Moon Goddess, from whom comes also that element in love which transcends the common workaday reality and connects the lovers with the gods themselves. Indeed, it was this very desire to attract which was the redeeming error that led Psyche, disobeying the prohibition of Aphrodite, to open the vial of beauty ointment she was bringing back from Persephone in order to make herself even more lovely for her beloved.

When the animus makes a woman insist upon being "just herself," she loses her magic. She remains only Miss or Mrs. So-and-So. She may be an excellent comrade, but the archetypal experience will not be found with her. There is a vast difference between the eros woman and the anima woman. The latter is just an empty little vessel, waiting to be filled up with the libido of the man, which she counts upon to supply her not inconsiderable demands on life, while the former is connected with her own feminine nature and its archetypal depths in such a way that the mystery and magic of life can live in her. She submits to the projection of the anima; she even makes it easy by enhancing every attribute God gave her, but without losing or falsifying herself.

The place of the archetypal roles in love is a subtle one, very difficult to describe, because the part consciousness can and should play depends upon the stage of development. First, nature is everything, the instincts dominate, and the archetypal patterns, out of sight in the undifferentiated matrix of the unconscious, make for the indefinite repetition of a stereotype. With the emergence of a separate ego, the pattern will be interfered with to some extent. It may be exploited for personal enjoyment or power or greed, and there comes a largely illusory sense of freedom, illusory because the purposes for which the archetype is exploited are no more truly free than was the functioning of instinct. The stage of the domination of impulse by an unenlightened ego is an inevitable phase, but it is still a bondage.

The next step in the growth of consciousness is the criticism of motives, and an attempt to sacrifice those acts which had been performed for regressive or unconscious reasons. But intellectual criticism is the bailiwick of the animus and often leads the newly self-conscious woman not only to reject the things that had been done as a means of "getting" the man, but also, on a deeper level, to try to get rid of all unconscious elements in the relationship. She not only refuses to make herself beautiful to please a man, but, much more damaging, tries to eliminate all the nonpersonal patterns and to function "just as herself."

Of course, it is a terrible ego inflation to imagine it is possible to abolish the effect of the archetypes in one's individual life. The person drowning in them or with only one eyebrow above water must struggle against them, but if the struggle is continued after the need is over it is at the expense of life. For the forces in the unconscious are the winds and currents to which we all must learn to adapt if we are to navigate our ship and not be the helpless sport of circumstances, inner and outer. So the next necessary step is for the woman to go beyond the need to be loved exclusively "just for herself," to the acceptance of the nonpersonal aspect of the experience also, which has very little to do with either of the participants.

Now it is apparent that the winds and tides of nonpersonal libido may be exceedingly powerful in the man-woman relation. This is especially true in the sex act itself, in which the personalities of the participants are momentarily suspended in an experience they share with all but the most primitive forms of life. The ego is pushed aside by the force of nature. Intercourse is not primarily an experience of personal love, as women try to make it, but of the gods, which yet happens through the union of the two. The love comes before, as a preparation, or after, as a result. But the love is then changed. The partner is no longer felt to be limited to the familiar conscious personality, but has become also the gateway to the infinite mystery of life. Projection? Yes, partly. Yet a projection that must be treated very tenderly, for it may lead to the most precious kind of love.

So we begin to see how, quite apart from the all-too-common duplicity and power in a woman's efforts to attract and hold men, there is also a secret art of knowing how the libido of two ordinary people can be freed to leap across the abyss of sexual polarity, so that each may, for a moment, find in the other not only a nice and dear person but the reflection of the soul itself. This art does not come from the strictly personal self of the woman but from the archetypal moon nature within, to which she becomes, as it were, mediumistic. This inner connection enables her to carry to some extent, or at least not reject, the role in which she may find herself cast in the eyes of her lover—as Eve or Helen of Troy, the Virgin Mary or Carmen—but without ever violating her own truth. If she has integrity, she will never enact these roles for the effect they produce, but her closer contact with the unconscious will make it possible for the man to find them in her because they are universal images which are potentially part of erotic experience and express the nonpersonal truth of a particular moment. The woman may make it easy or very hard for the man to touch these depths with her.

You will have no illusion that this depth of awareness in the love experience is at all common. I am speaking here of the woman who has passed through the phase of collecting the projections of men, has, perhaps, revolted indiscriminately against the things she had done in that stage in an effort to get a more real and personal relationship, but has finally come to see in the unconscious the nonpersonal, organic patterns of life which are constellated in the relation and may greatly enrich it. She began as the anima woman, reflecting the feelings of the man instead of relating to them, went on to finding her own true reactions and the inner patterns from which they sprang, and finally was able, through this connection with her collective roots, to become the mediator between the man and the collective unconscious, which, as anima holder, she had previously been only in a blind, instinctive way.

Thus the transcendence of the anima woman may lead to the true eros woman, who stands half in the light and half in darkness and unites the two. This kind of feminine consciousness is still very rare, but its development has been made more possible by the methods of Jung's depth psychology. Only at this stage is it possible for a woman to move with the lines of force of collective patterns without the danger of losing herself. One starts in the womb of autonomous, archetypal life. One ends in a return to the unconscious, this time in freedom and with vision and a gay humorousness.

The archetypal yin wants to submit in love. So it is not necessarily an overadaptation to the man or a falsification of herself when a woman submits. But it must be to something worthwhile in him, not to mere masculine vanity or ego power. For the submissiveness of the woman stands over against her independence in a theoretically irreconcilable conflict. It can remain one of the many paradoxes of the Self unless it is inflamed by the man's arbitrary or exploitative attitude. Then the gentler side will disappear, perhaps forever.

Now let us turn to the two other figures in the relationship drama—the man and his anima. As in the case of the woman, what purports to be just himself turns out to have an archetypal side too, standing close behind him, the hero or wise old man. As he constellates this archetype for the woman, so bringing to life her feminine charm and womanliness, so she holds the reciprocal function for him. When he is with her, powers come alive in him that he did not know he possessed. The fact that she is able to see, to respond to, even almost to worship, the masculine principle, the logos, which he represents to her, may make some latent spark of the hero or wise man glow within him, so that he feels himself to be truly more than he had been without her. This enhances his conscious self, leading to inflation in the unwary, but to the fulfillment of hitherto slumbering potentialities in a man great souled enough to be humble.

Here, it seems to me, there is a difference between the reactions of men and women. The man fulfilled in love goes forth to meet the world with new joy and confidence. While the woman, being more conscious in the realm of eros, may stay at home and give her attention to herself, he must not. She may make herself attractive physically, and also prepare psychologically for his coming by getting herself into the free and undistracted state of mind in which life is apt to flow most strongly. She is right in doing this, because she knows it is something quite other than the ego she is invoking. In the love situation, the man pursues, so his eye is naturally on the object. But the woman must bring him to her by something within herself if there is to be any relation at all. The man seeks the woman with need and love and longing and she connects him, if it is in her, with the stores of nourishment from the Great Mother of life.

If woman is the psychological sex—because her feminine nature is closer to the unconscious—then it is one of her most precious gifts to be able to open for herself and for the one she loves the channels to the springs of life in the unconscious. In the simple, primitive sort of woman, this happens naturally. But as people's lives become crowded with the aims and activities of personal existence, the well-springs get blocked, the waters dammed up, and the "wastelands" come into being. This is the great danger to the emotional life of the business or professional woman. She, too, risks developing the atti-tude of the famous, or infamous, "tired business man," jaded, hun-gry and in need of being filled up. When that happens to her, almost any man will turn to the child-woman instead, because the very naivete of such a one releases the flow of natural instinctive life and relieves his sense of stalemate, even though her immaturity makes her unable to meet him except on the most primitive and undeveloped side of himself. In this way his anima may become split, represented by a presentable companion-woman on the one hand and an impor-tant, though often rather despised, infantile plaything on the other.

The correspondence between these two sides of the man's split anima and the animus and anima types of women have led some people to blame women entirely for the generally low level of eros in our civilization, and for the anima difficulties of men in particular. But it is foolish to blame either half of the population for a phe-nomenon of the times in which both sexes have obviously had a hand. One could as truly say that the animus revolt of women was caused by the split anima which often made the man such an inade-quate lover that the woman became starved and restless. But it is to be hoped that most people will refrain from such futile arguing in a circle, and try instead to break somewhere into the vicious alternation of action and reaction which has brought us to our present pass. And here and there I think this is actually beginning to happen. For, while men struggle with their own special problems in science, finance and world politics, watched and often abetted by women, the latter are discovering that something can be done in their native realm of eros to reintegrate the ways of nature and effect the archetypal union of yang and yin in conscious human experience. Here the man can only stand by and abet her. This subject will be further elaborated in the chapter on friendship.

In his relation to a woman, a man's masculine side is constellated. He is the wooer, the active pursuer; he carries her away. But the process going on in him is less self-conscious, less carefully prepared, than that taking place in her. The Chinese say that the movement of yang progresses in space; that of yin is an opening and closing.

The anima is experienced at first only in projection onto a woman, who, like the man's mother before her, is expected to fill his every physical and emotional need. If she refuses to do so, she becomes a Lilith in his eyes, frustrating him and throwing him from one mood to another. But presently he may begin to discover that these moods of his tell more about himself than they do about his partner. And that, of course, is the beginning of wisdom.

The fact that the anima always holds something of the mother at the start makes the man, who then feels himself to be a child, both vulnerable and demanding. Yet without the projection of the anima, whatever she may be like, his relation to the woman remains superficial. The psychological peril of falling under the maternal spell must be risked, for only so can it be overcome. The man who fears to get caught emotionally will not get very far in an eros situation. But when he finds all his heart's desire in projected form he may realize his own capacity to react with true feeling, which in turn creates an atmosphere in which the woman can thrive. She blossoms in the sunshine of his love, becoming more alive, more fulfilled and ever more beautiful because of it. And as the relation progresses, the anima may be transformed into the subjective function of sensibility and creative feeling.

There is nothing to be gained by trying to avoid the complications of love by staying uninvolved. Esther Harding speaks of the ability to bear the impact of strong emotion as one form of initiation into eros. She cites the myth of Isis, who took the child Maneros into the boat with her with the intent of bestowing immortality upon him.[35] But in the night she made her lamentations for her slain spouse Osiris. The grief of the goddess was terrible to see, and the little boy, unable to stand it, fell overboard. That is, he protected himself from emotion by becoming unconscious, which is death, and, of course, in this way lost all chance of immortality.

Deep emotion, as opposed to mere emotionality, comes from the nonpersonal unconscious, so it may suitably be pictured as a goddess. There is a vast number of men these days, as well as a few women, who try to escape it like the plague. For example, a man who had had quite a lot of analysis came to me one day complaining of severe nausea and other symptoms of indigestion, which he suspected was psychogenic, though he could find no adequate explanation. So I began to dig around and soon unearthed these facts. The man, a widower, had been seeing a great deal of an unhappily married lady of whom he was quite enamored, and they had discussed the possibility of her getting a divorce to marry him. She could not make up her mind, and, as she had been having severe bronchitis anyway, decided to go south for the winter to think it over. He agreed that that would be a very valuable thing for both of them. She was to depart in a couple of days. So far he had taken her prospective absence with the most coolly rational equanimity. But—he became terribly nauseous.

On discussing the situation, and after I had asked a lot of leading questions, he admitted he would be lonely and miserable without her and that the months ahead looked like a dreary waste when he tried to visualize them. He did then accept the impact of the emotion, and he had no more nausea. And incidentally he was able to say good-by to her with an unprecedented intensity, which made a bond that lasted during her absence. They were married as soon after her return as she could get her divorce.

There is a long short story called *The Beast in the Jungle* by Henry James that portrays with marvelous insight a man who simply could not give any allegiance to the emotional side of life, and the consequence to himself. He was in love with a charming and devoted

---

[35] *Woman's Mysteries*, p. 174.

woman and they were expecting to get married in a short time. But one evening he arrived as usual at her home, saying that he had something very serious to tell her, and that, though it affected drastically all their plans, the strange thing was that he could not even say what it was. All he knew was that it had suddenly come to him, in a flash of inexorable certainty, that he was marked for some terrible fate, which, like a beast in the jungle, would leap upon him without warning and destroy him. Knowing this beyond the shadow of a doubt, he could not in decency, he said, ask anyone, least of all the woman he loved, to share such a fate.

In vain she protested that he could not prevent her sharing it because she loved him. Anything that happened to him was in her fate too. He was nobly adamant; he would not allow it. But he did not in the least relax his claim upon her time; he continued to spend his evenings with her, passed mostly in eternal discussions and conjectures about what this strange and interesting fate could be, which made him such a tragic and appealing figure, in his own eyes as well as hers. He seemed to thrive on this sort of thing, though she didn't. She became pale and drawn, lost weight and vitality, and finally died. He was appropriately grief-stricken and could not understand why the family did not include him among the chief mourners at the funeral. Nevertheless, he made it his practice thereafter to go to the cemetery regularly every Sunday afternoon to lay a little flower on her grave. One day as he entered the cemetery to perform this ritual he came face to face with a man just turning away from a newly made grave. The man's expression was one of such stark, irretrievably tragic loss that our hitherto complacent hero suddenly knew that the beast had sprung. It was the realization that he had never in all his life loved anyone but himself enough to suffer as much as that. And so the evaded or outraged forces of the unconscious hold always the last card.

Life cannot be cheated, however plausible the excuse seems to be. It does not require a belief in reincarnation to see the ineluctable truth of karma—that life is real and absolutely everything we do, whether knowingly or not, affects what we become. And so the people, and as we have seen, especially often the men who want the pleasures of love without any serious commitment, miss out in the end. And incidentally there is a curious little fact here. The person who is not serious in love or in any other situation of importance is the one who cannot really play either. He is only frivolous, fooling around, joshing, "killing time." We can imagine the man in James's story being frightfully solemn, though he was not really serious; he could probably indulge in games and recreational activities, but never go along with the gay, joyous, irrational flow of life.

However inevitable is the stage of the projection of animus and anima, it cannot be a satisfactory state permanently in a growing personality. The apparent effort of these powerful archetypes to break into, and control, reality by forcing the partner to enact a role produces a game between the sexes that is dangerously akin to war. Each attempts to whittle the actual shape of the other to fit his or her own need or wish. This secret power clinch becomes a struggle almost to the death. In the end, the man may turn into a regular Bluebeard in his effort to dominate. The woman's power is more subtle and regularly masquerades under the guise of the mother. An extraordinary instance of this is given in a story of a Borgia princess who is said to have poured a drop of poison, night by night, into her lover's soup, and, day by day, received the wonder and admiration of the court by wearing herself to skin and bone taking care of him. But she had to reduce him to being all hers, just like a helpless child, before she would pour out her tenderness upon him.

The worst snarls in relationships between men and women are certainly caused by the entanglement of animus and anima. When a man has no conscious contact with his anima, he has to force the woman to *be* his inner image in order to experience his positive feeling at all. Often he expects her to be ready to receive him at any hour of the day or night, according to his whim; and she must not mind being laid on the shelf afterward if he has other interests afoot, with no word from him until the mood for a little lovemaking seizes him again. Thus he compels her to be the mere reflection of his own capricious feeling and denies her a vote in the common concerns of the relationship. And woe be to her if she responds with any sort of claim on his time. The one thing he cannot do is to take her as she is, a separate personality, for the anima is always a somewhat mythologized version of a real woman. He becomes irritable and feels insecure if she does not carry, at least passively, the role he wants from her. She in turn is apt to react to this perhaps unspoken expectation or demand by a wordy defensiveness, telling him her opinion of him with a speciousness peculiarly hard to refute. She hits upon a weak spot and then ties him up in verbiage. In the ensuing struggle he grows petulant and childish, she hard, legalistic and unreachable. Her superior, bossy attitude infuriates him, and his consequent emotionality further convinces her that she is the reasonable one while he is just being uncontrolled and difficult.

If they could but see that this is all the doing of the secret actors behind their backs—her inferior masculine side and his inferior feminine side—if he could remember that she is the woman he loves, even if she is not built on the pattern of his personal specifications, and if she could realize that she might get somewhere by reacting from her heart instead of treating him to the frigidity of her opinionated animus, then the deadlock could almost certainly be released. If they could only behold each other in the light, as Psyche succeeded in doing, mindful of all the values they share, instead of passively standing by while animus and anima engage in a free-for-all, they could work through to some understanding and mutual acceptance. True relationship must always involve separate individuals, and it is not natural or possible that they should agree on everything. Yang and yin are fundamentally opposed principles, inexorably tied together, yet inexorably at war, until a superior point of reconciliation is achieved. This miracle is made possible by love.

Of course, the animus may be the one to precipitate the conflict. It may lead the woman to tell the man what he ought to do, or make some generalized assumption that to him is obviously invalid yet upon which she pontificates with the most maddening assurance. This unrelated pseudo-thinking chills the atmosphere, producing an alienation of feeling which is greatly worsened by the dictatorial manner in which the pronouncements are made. Thus the two human beings do not touch each other at all, but become separated by a thick barrier of immovable thoughts and feelings through which they cannot hear each other speak.

Illustrations of the way these unconscious figures interpose themselves between two people are so ubiquitous that perhaps it is unnecessary to give any others. Yet we are all so liable to get caught by them that it may be worthwhile to give one more. Here a young wife had been brought up in a family in which birthdays were considered as very important occasions. Her father had always brought her mother flowers on that day, and usually there had been some little party, a special dinner and perhaps a trip to the theater. So when her first birthday after the wedding came round and no mention was made of the occasion, she was deeply hurt and felt that her husband was losing interest in her, oblivious of the fact that it is a pure assumption that birthdays must necessarily be celebrated. In the husband's large family of many brothers and sisters, no attention had been paid to them and so he was completely unaware of having failed her in any way. He felt she was unfairly critical and disparaging of his real affection. Moreover, her attitude made it impossible for him to accept her point of view with any cordiality or enthusiasm, as she easily might have enabled him to do if she had expressed her desire amicably, instead of first putting him in the wrong. Trivial? Yes, certainly, but the sort of thing that I have seen cause a ridiculous amount of unhappiness.

I once knew a marriage that nearly went on the rocks because of the passion that got into a discussion over whether a Pekingese or a Pomeranian was the nicer breed of dog. Of course, the real issue was the wife's right to have an opinion that differed from her husband's, but this could not be realized as long as they talked about dogs. There the animus could steal the emotion from the two important matters involved, namely, their love for each other and the necessity to disidentify. The woman's expectation in the birthday incident, that her husband would be the kind of mate to her that her father had been to her mother, is also a very common form of animus assumption. It is the carry-over of the child's idea that its parents are the best model for the way things should be. Until it is relinquished, she will either be childishly demanding and so alienate her partner, or she will just be hurt, and, though she may decide to suffer in silence, the first brick will have been laid in a barrier between them that will eventually shut off all real communication.

On the man's side, a lack of immediate sexual response from his bride, which he feels to be a deliberate rejection, is often the thing which irritates the anima. In our civilization an immediate and mutual sexual adjustment is by no means the rule, especially, I fear, with highly educated women. Frequently it is necessary for the man to have great patience while his young wife finds the way into the instinctual depths of her nature. If for this reason, or because of fatigue or emotional strain, she is at times unresponsive to his advances, he feels inferior and resentful and thinks she does not really love him. He may then become sulky and again a drifting apart ensues. If these difficulties can be faced squarely between them, they can usually be overcome. But if the critical animus and the resentful anima remain in the saddle, the situation goes from bad to worse until it becomes irremediable.

Anima and animus, when in control, always act in such a way as to entirely isolate their victims, like a jealous lover who tries to cut off any relationship which might threaten exclusive possession. The individual thus possessed either cannot care greatly for anyone or makes such an unrealistic transference, involving such fantastic expectations, that it is sure to crash, leaving the person once more isolated. If one then tries to restore the broken rapport by apparently giving up the exaggerated claims without really coming to terms with the underlying animus or anima problem, the capitulation all too often turns out to be only a falsification of the situation, hiding the still undissipated resentment under a placating mask of compliance.

The inability of people to meet as they really are is the theme of a play by Eugene O'Neill, *The Great God Brown*, in which most of the characters put on masks whenever they are not alone. Here the husband, really a shy and sensitive lad with a great feeling of inferiority, compensates by wearing a mask of a somewhat truculent assurance. Under its protection, he treats his employer with a foolishly aggressive defiance, which quite naturally loses him his job. To his wife, however, for whom he is, at the beginning of their marriage, the dauntless hero, this defensive brashness looks like high-spirited courage in the face of a veritable old dragon of a boss. Several times he tries to remove his mask when he is with her, but her look of blank, incredulous dismay forces him to resume it in haste, though he is actually suffocating under the false role of the young hero.

Only two people in the play do not have to wear masks. One is the wife while she is still projecting onto her husband and is consequently still shut up in the egg, living securely in a world so entirely populated by the figures she sees painted on the inside of the shell that even her most sensitive feelings need no defense. The other is the village harlot, who is portrayed as the polar opposite of the wife.

She is a woman with the all-accepting nature of the earth itself, completely without illusions, who takes men exactly as they are. She needs neither an illusory protection nor an illusory charm, for she is able to give them what they need through her wide humanity and her deep contact with the instinctual springs of life.

In the realm of love, the words of Walt Whitman are particularly appropriate: "Only the kernel nourishes." Only those human beings who bring their deepest inmost reality to love will have any share in its true joy and fulfillment. This is too often forgotten by young people who think they know the truth about love because they have had a fine salad of erotic experience. Actually what they cynically call their realism is only a cloak for a complete ignorance of everything below the surface. They have been too greedy for pleasure, too unwilling to face pain, or just too unawakened to stand up against the momentary drift in their social set ever to be able to deserve anything but the anger of the god of love. As Kahlil Gibran says in *The Prophet*:

> For even as love crowns you, so shall he crucify you.
> * * * * * * * *
> He threshes you to make you naked.
> He sifts you to free you from husks.
> He grinds you to whiteness.
> He kneads you till you are pliant.
> * * * * * * * *
> But if, in your fear, you would seek only love's peace
>   and love's pleasure,
> Then it is better for you that you cover your nakedness and
>   pass out of love's threshing-floor,
> Into the seasonless world where you shall laugh, but not all
>   of your laughter, and weep, but not all of your tears.[36]

Of course, the problem of men and women boils down to the development of human relationship and the ability to love. When two people fall in love, they are not yet truly loving but are caught in a tidal wave of nature which, for the time being, lifts them up and hurls them together. But it will just as surely set them down again in disillusionment, unless, in the moment of togetherness, they have

---

[36] Kahlil Gibran, *The Prophet* (New York: Alfred A. Knopf, Inc., 1923).

built a solid bridge of communication and relatedness. For modern men and women this must be a new kind of relationship, one which incorporates whatever increase of consciousness has been achieved during this era of struggle and transition. In the past, more had to be left to unaided nature; and since nature in the psyche, as well as elsewhere, is split into a multitude of opposing forces, this *laissez aller* attitude, except insofar as it was held in check by convention or religion, meant the dominance of now this, now that, natural or semirationalized impulse. One's fate has been, to a considerable extent, determined by such one-sided drives. Either one was lucky in love or not. The god of love was indeed a blind little fellow, and not only blind but often thoroughly mischievous to boot. Yet while this almost accidental character of love is a fact, we have come to realize how closely accident is related to the unconscious, and consequently that it is also a fact that the kind of relationship of which a person is capable is determined by the kind of person one is. Just here comes in a small element of freedom from the chance arrows of the god.

I remember the enormous impression made upon me some years ago by the man-made lightning shown in the electric exhibit at the World's Fair in New York. This consisted of millions of volts sent roaring and crackling from one electric pole to another. To me that powerful blue streak was a symbol of the superhuman energy of the unleashed forces of the collective unconscious. As I watched, spellbound and in awe, it became the image of the overwhelming emotions that may be constellated between a fragile human man and woman. It pictured the incalculable energy of the instincts and archetypes in violent interaction. This is something quite beyond the small sphere controlled by the human will. It belongs to the drama of the gods or cosmic forces.

The poles through which the torrential energy flows, however, are human business. If either of them is shoddy or should fuse under the impact of such a current, not only would the pole be destroyed forever, but the whole dynamic process would be stopped short and turned to disaster. In early maturity the man and woman who are the poles are too soft, too childish, too greedy and ignorant to be able to carry on a relation of great intensity without danger of cracking if something goes wrong. They may fear it, especially if they have once been burned, and try to keep the involvement light in every way they can. But usually they are more naive and fall into it before they realize what is happening. Then they will throw themselves upon each other for support. In that case one or the other of them is apt, sooner or later, to feel this to be too much, and to try to withdraw. For it is indeed a stern fate to be the medium through which the lightning elects to flow. Yet it is just that fate that has compelled many a young person to make the ascent from psychological childhood to maturity. The energy of intense desire either turns destructive or is made to heat the retort for the alchemical transformation. I have seen many a person who had been a spoiled and self-indulgent darling of the parents develop through such an experience into a serious and responsible adult, able to take whatever gambles were required in the relationship, and to pay the stakes if necessary. One does not expect to command the lightning, but one may reasonably aspire to carry oneself appropriately in a thunderstorm.

Perhaps the supreme expression of the daemonic, force-of-nature character of erotic love has been given by Wagner in his *Tristan and Isolde*. There the irresistible flood of passion sweeps aside all ordinary human values and the lovers—their individual wills helpless against it—are inexorably rushed toward death, the only possible outcome. To justify their complete absorption in this one-sided drive, regardless of Tristan's personal knightly duty to King Mark, Wagner introduces the motif of the love potion, pure magic, which abrogates the power of the conscious will.

This symbolizes perfectly the sort of glamorous spell under which lovers seem to live. But this unfree condition is felt by some people, especially men, to be somehow unclean, for in it their logos side is swamped. They feel that way, perhaps I should rather say, after they come out of it. While they are still under its influence, they glorify everything about it, which they see as bathed in a radiantly rosy light. The wise man, like Merlin, willingly loses his wisdom, for awhile! But as the glamour wanes, previous moral considerations and responsibilities are suddenly remembered; with a sigh of relief, the husbands return to the status of respectable citizens, and happily take up life again with wife and kids. If love is extramarital, it had better be interesting, for when it palls, even ever so little, the man will begin to discover his conscience and then the game is up. Actually the man is never comfortable for long in a too intense eros situation, for his anima takes over and, like Merlin in the toils of Vivien, he may lose his independence and be paralyzed all the rest of his life. But women love it and flourish like the green bay tree. In spite of the inevitably tragic ending of a completely daemonic love, some women enjoy enacting the part, and, by identifying with Isolde or Heloise or another of the great sisterhood, inflate their very commonplace little affairs with an importance which in no wise belongs to them. This happens when the animus devours the nonpersonal factor. Then the situation becomes just a passionately blown-up idea of love, sexuality in the head, as it is often expressed in dreams. In such a case the woman is desirous, jealous, possessive and altogether compulsive toward the man. There is no warmth in it, no real rapport or flow of life. A purely physical attraction, which is real enough, may underlie the situation, but surprisingly often even this may exist mostly in the woman's imagination. It is a sort of scheme or plot of the animus, which, having clamped down on a particular man, practically commandeers him for the purpose of propelling her into the fascinating and dramatic current of erotic life. Just as the child can quite safely play the hero, so all sorts of secret desires and flimsy claims can masquerade as *grandes passions*. But in fact the latter game is not safe either, for it is possible to be more hellishly involved by power than by love, and with more disastrous consequences. The real lover always gains something, but the one seeking power loses all.

Love is not necessarily shared equally by both partners, greatly as this is to be desired. The lives of most men are too taken up with the concerns of the world for them to have enough time or energy left over to make good lovers. Usually they marry and settle down to a comfortably unconscious home life, in which their wives are expected to be three-quarters mother. That isn't very exciting, though safe and fairly pleasant, so they will fill the gap by an occasional leap over the wall of matrimony into an affair, which, however, they are too moral to take seriously. The woman who wants to drink deep of love will find few men able and willing to companion her. Yet, if the man is reasonably considerate and amounts to something in his own world, he may be the partner in an experience, which, for her, is a veritable initiation into the mystery of her own emotional nature.

But the experience, first of her intensity and then of renunciation, will be hard for her and involve much suffering. Nevertheless, I have known only one woman who, having lived such an experience through with the best she had to give, would wish it never to have been. For from it comes lasting self-knowledge, and it may so connect her with her own emotional depths that she will be wise with woman's wisdom long after the man has gone his way. But she may also have to recognize that the majority of so-called love affairs are pretty banal when all is said and done, just two people brought together for a moment of pleasure or escape, if not for more sordid and cynical motives. A woman will hate to admit this, especially if it concerns herself, and will be likely to lay the blame on the man's more physical urgency and what she considers his more frivolous attitude. With her eye full of this she will probably not ask herself what she is prepared to bring to the relationship other than a mass of unfulfilled hopes and desires.

The woman who is well versed in the ways of eros will hold herself open to the irrational currents of the moment, so that the unexpected may happen at any time. This keeps things alive and free from the deadening effects of habit, like intercourse by the alarm clock Sunday mornings. But above all, she will be oriented to the man and will really desire to follow in the direction he sets, because she realizes that her own deepest satisfaction comes when she has brought out the truly masculine in him and then follows his lead.

It seems to me that the dance is a most apt illustration of the man-woman relation. He sets the pace, takes the lead. But her role is no less difficult or creative. Her body and her intuition are completely responsive to the least move he makes. The two roles are equally essential to a beautiful and creative whole. But when this interaction is a matter of their lives and not only of a few moments of delightful recreation, it is important that he should be worthy of his position of leadership. For, as was said at the beginning, it is not his vanity and egotism that she can gladly follow. When these predominate, she must try to find a way to get past the obstruction they cause between them, but subtly, without making an issue of it, and in no case critically or in a superior manner. For her position toward him is not one of teacher or judge but of a loving human being struggling to conserve the thing she most values in life, the rapport with her man. The tendency always is to summon the animus to fight for her, which makes her tackle a delicate situation with a sledgehammer, or, worse still, with a poison dart.

We have seen how talk motivated by the animus makes men shy away from discussing intimate problems. They fear, and with good reason, the power of the animus to tie them up in words that do not convince, but which they are quite unable to refute; for their masculine logic would be impotent in an eros situation, even if the woman's animus did not so invariably hammer away at something slightly, maddeningly, beside the point. So he will give her instead a little absent treatment, a thing anathema to her. He will leave her strictly alone until he believes she has capitulated, or at least until the problem has become sufficiently nebulous to be passed over in silence. He can turn more easily to affairs outside the sphere of eros and forget it, as the woman cannot do without leaving her heart, and so her very self, behind. Or worst of all, he can seek comfort in the arms of another, which will usually bring the first lady around. That something precious has been wounded by his attitude does not enter his head. The greater centeredness of the woman's eros makes her really suffer from the dislocation until it is cured. The man, too, will usually admit, after the reconciliation, that the sense of release it brings is amply worth the cost of facing the problem frankly. But before the woman can hope to induce him to stay with it long enough to get it settled, she must make him feel that she has no ax of ego power to grind, that she is seeking only to free their relation from stoppage, and that she is quite as willing to admit it when she is in the wrong as to convict him.

In the same way that the woman who is to follow the lead of her man gladly must be able to feel that he represents for her the masculine sense of truth and justice, so the man who is to risk what might be called his "sensitive underbelly" of anima feeling in articulate exchange with a woman must trust the disinterestedness of her motives and her gentleness in touching painful spots. For such discussions may be acutely painful for both parties, and much devotion and tact is required to make a renewed rapport emerge from a situation that started as a threat. Only a series of such experiences can prove the individual character of the relationship. Until an imminent collision has been averted by mutual understanding and the acceptance of differences, one cannot be sure how much the love depends upon a tissue of projection and illusion rather than upon reality.

Though the exercise of this art of maintaining a rapport is the particular responsibility—or privilege—of women, its success depends equally on the moral caliber of both partners. In developing a conscious relationship, the woman will need the yin qualities of pliancy and devotion, but the yang qualities of clarity and independence are also essential. Obviously she can accomplish little alone. If the man is not deeply involved with her, he will lose interest rather than face anything that might prove difficult or unpleasant. But if his love is strong, then she has a real chance to foster the bit of life between them that can grow to be uniquely theirs, and hence so irreplaceable that no newcomer is likely to be able to undermine the union.

It should be recognized that this is as great and creative an accomplishment as writing a book or painting a picture. The medium is not ink or pigment but the very fabric of human life. And most men I have talked with who have had the experience of an individual relationship willingly admit that it was thanks to the love and tact of the woman. Here it is that she makes her unique contribution. And this means more than the outer achievement, because the consciousness of those concerned evolves with the relationship, slowly gaining breadth and solidity and form. Thus, the work upon the relationship in itself helps the lovers to become the unfusible human poles we spoke of, capable of carrying a much stronger current of life than before. Clearly, if life is meant to be fully lived, this is a furtherance of its purpose; for the higher the voltage that the carriers can bear without disintegrating, the deeper is the experience. The urgent masculine sexual impulse furnishes the drive, and the feminine power of nurture and conservation gives it enduring effect. In the relation the woman comes to realize that there is more to a sexual union than the love of a personal object, and the man finds that the releasing effect which he needs is greatly enhanced, at least in the long run, when there is a foundation of deep and tested love.

These observations lead to the conclusion that the desire of the man for a moment of complete fulfillment with the woman is, *au fond*, a longing for an experience of the nonpersonal libido. The woman, on the other hand, in striving for permanence with a particular man, is seeking personal relatedness. The former is, as a consequence, oriented to the electric current, the latter to the poles. But the current is impossible without the poles; the poles meaningless without the current. The man and woman must each bow to the utter indispensability of the complementary principle in the other, while firmly maintaining one's own. The woman who takes sexuality on the same easy, impersonal basis as the man fails to hold up the feminine side, and so the potential drops. For if the poles are the same, both positive or both negative, no current will flow. Similarly, the man who is so tied to one woman that he cannot see any other is apt to become quite a bore, even to the lady of his choice. And so again the current fails. For its existence there must be an adequate difference of potential, or, in psychological terms, a strong yang-yin polarization. If a spirited woman is to be fired enough to follow a man's lead devotedly, she must see in him a true spark of the creative masculine quality, and he must be able to carry something of this archetype without being puffed up or identified with it. And likewise the woman must allow the man to find in her the repose and renewal of the earth principle and the delicate colorfulness of that of the moon. Then he can bring to her his deepest reality, for she stimulates his strength but also accepts his weakness.

A man once asked his beloved: "Why do you care for me so much? Is it for my clever mind and the books I have written?" Her answer was that of a real woman, "Not a bit! I love you because you are such an old stupid!" Thus she playfully deflected the conversation from flattery of his ego to the deeper truth that love is not for personal assets or qualities, but for the being of the beloved. Had there been no basis of respect, she could not have answered that way without giving offense. But when there is, the human weaknesses may be more endearing than the strength.

This brings us to the two elements which I consider absolutely fundamental to individual relatedness, but which will be only mentioned here, for they are not especially characteristic of the man-woman relationship as over against all others. They are, first, acceptance and, second, trust. They will be discussed at more length in the chapter on friendship, but are mentioned here so that the reader may fill in this subject with that material when we come to it.

What does characterize the man-woman relation specifically is that through it both of them are led to an awareness and acceptance of the animus or anima, the function of relation to the unconscious. In giving up her self-will and submitting to the man she loves, the woman is led to a submission to an inner truth of her own nature. And in giving up his lust for freedom and settling down to one central relationship, the man is enabled to experience the eros in his own soul.

In the course of an analysis it is possible to witness the change in the quality of the animus or anima as the person develops. For example, a woman once came to me after working for some time with a male analyst. She was a professional woman whose instinctual side was like a healthy animal shut up in the cage made by her conventional upbringing. The result was that the animal was ravenous and terribly crude and primitive. The male analyst told her that what she needed was some sexual experience with men, and she should go get it. At that point he went away to a distant city, leaving her to dig up the men. There was no difficulty in doing this, but the sort of messes she got herself into with them left her torn between shame and a sort of illicit glee. There was simply no meeting point between her conscious and her unconscious. Also she had the most distressing dreams, full of sexual situations with men who were not sound, decent people, but dirty, diseased, sinister creatures that made her shiver. I saw this as her unconscious reaction to the advice of her analyst—who incidentally was not a Jungian—which might well have ended in her destruction.

No woman would think that mere sexuality would be any use for a woman if it were not integrated with her heart and her moral attitude. This does not mean that puritanism and prudery should remain entrenched, but to tear down an old morality on the strength of a transference to the analyst, and before the rudiments of a new one had appeared, was to my mind a criminal misuse of the analyst's function. Fortunately, her fundamental decency saved her. It was most interesting to watch the gradual improvement that took place in the sort of men appearing in her dreams. They ceased to be evil or pathological and became less primitive, until they finally appeared as truly cultured gentlemen. Then she had this dream:

> I saw a face of shining bronze with shining eyes looking at me. At first I thought he was laughing at me. I looked at him with serious intensity and realized that he was not laughing. As our eyes met, I knew that he understood me, but to me he was impenetrable. I awoke deeply moved.

She wrote of this:

My first idea on waking was that he was a Negro because of his dark skin, and I was annoyed that he seemed to be laughing at me. But this thought gave way to what I felt was the deeper import of the dream, suggested by the shining countenance and the depth of understanding in the eyes. I could think only of a Hindu god or a Buddha. Then again the Negro became quite clear. Finally that face seemed to me to unite God and devil, good and evil. But as the days wore on, it was the quality of infinite understanding that stayed with me.

The dream came the night after seeing again, after years of separation, one of the lovers of the messy stage of her life. He said that he had tried to get in touch with her, but she had moved several times and he had not been able to find her until now. He naturally expected to go on with the old type of relation, but when he found her unwilling he did not lose interest, only asked if he might see her when next he could get to New York. And she found herself reacting to him in a much more genuine way. She had changed and this worked a change in him. She had realized, as the dream shows, that the god of instinct, symbolized by the Negro, is also the one found in deepest introversion, the Buddha, and that life and its meaning are one. Whether it appears as god or devil depends upon one's attitude.

Thus, the sexual union is fundamentally symbolic and this is its deepest meaning. It expresses the *coniunctio,* that mystic inner marriage which was the goal of the alchemical work. By its process Sol and Luna, gold and silver, logos and eros, were no longer to be estranged but united.

A strong, clear projection is essential before the assimilation of an unconscious content is possible. Until it has been made, the whole drama takes place out of sight in the unconscious and acts upon the ego from behind, in the manner of a suggestion made under hypnosis which is carried out after the trance is ended. The visible effect of a positive erotic projection is to draw the man and woman together; then it is up to them whether they make a real relationship out of its energy. But even if successfully accomplished, this is only one side of the possible end result. The other is that wholeness should emerge from the identification by, in Jung's words,

the conscious union of the ego with everything that has been projected into the "You." Hence wholeness is the product of an intrapsychic process which depends essentially on the relation of one individual to another. Relationship paves the way for individuation and makes it possible, but is itself no proof of wholeness.[37]

Jung says further that "without the conscious acknowledgement and acceptance of our fellowship with those around us there can be no synthesis of personality."[38] And again:

> Individuation has two principal aspects: in the first place it is an internal and subjective process of integration, and in the second it is an equally indispensable process of objective relationship. Neither can exist without the other, although sometimes the one and sometimes the other predominates.[39]

The *coniunctio* is, of course, a completely nonpersonal process, as separate from the ego of the individual in whom it takes place as is the flash of lightning from the electric pole which may appear to give it rise. Yet the individual must be able to endure the fire. Jung says that the integration of the unconscious is possible only if the ego holds its ground. In the *coniunctio*, love and truth are reconciled. The woman adores the spirit embodied for her in the man, and he in turn comes to realize that spirit must incarnate as love. So the human union is paralleled and completed by the mystic marriage of the opposite principles within the psyche.

This rarely happens consciously, yet back of the relations of a man and a woman, there lies in the unconscious the image of this transcendent union, waiting to be wakened into life. Though a really complete relationship is a great and rare achievement, success in the outer sphere is not necessary to bring about the inner result; nor is the outer success of a happy marriage, in itself, any guarantee that a high psychological goal has been attained. Indeed, it is a striking fact that frustration seems to be the fate of most great lovers. Perhaps this is more often the case in literature than in life, due to the needs of the plot for suffering and struggle. Yet my observation has not led me to be too sanguine about real life in this respect. Perhaps just the suffer-

---

[37] "The Psychology of the Transference," *The Practice of Psychotherapy,* CW 16, par. 454, note 16.

[38] Ibid., par. 444.

[39] Ibid., par. 448.

ing and the struggle are the *conditio sine qua non,* the vital condition, for the production of redeemed love or the philosophers' gold.

The alchemists sometimes advised the use of a gentle heat on the retort, which would correspond to brooding or introverting. But sometimes the directions called for the application of intense heat. The psychological equivalent of this could hardly be less than the full intensity of passionate conflict and emotion, and passion mounts when it meets a barrier. Indeed, the libido tries so frantically to fulfill itself in outer reality that it can hardly be made to turn inward to create a psychological value unless it has come up against an impenetrable wall. Then it is forced back upon itself. Only then, if at all, does the alchemical process begin.

That both partners in a love relation should be able and willing to follow the intensities constellated between them into the shadowy world of the soul, and there to share the alchemical quest for the indestructible while at the same time sharing a satisfactory home life, is far too improbable to expect. Indeed, I doubt whether it is possible until life has awakened them by some severe blow. But whether in the form of fulfillment or frustration, life in some form has knocked at everyone's door, and from it an inner treasure may have been garnered, even when the outer fruit seemed pretty small. The power of Saturn, the Frustrater, is nowhere more destructive, or, at times, more ultimately beneficent, than in the realm of love.[40]

The woman who has become conscious realizes that eros is always important in her life, and she will take with inner seriousness her relationships, particularly those with men, because of the contact with the gods, the suprapersonal forces of the unconscious that may flow through them. But she will learn to distinguish the situations in which the gods are at play from those of more serious import. In the former case, she, too, will play, yet she will be careful to keep even those small relations clear and true, so that their nature will be understood and accepted by both parties. She will also learn to be able to carry herself and not lean too heavily on her partner. Men usually hate to have affairs taken too solemnly. One man I know said to his lover, "For heaven's sake, don't make a great spiritual experience

---

[40] [These issues are explored at length in Aldo Carotenuto, *Eros and Pathos: Shades of Love and Suffering* (Toronto: Inner City Books, 1989.—Ed.]

out of this." As a matter of fact, that particular relation, though light enough on the surface, proved to be a very significant landmark in her life, but that side of it she had to carry alone, always meeting the man with a lightness of touch that would not scare him off. That took a really gallant spirit on her part, incidentally. It is only when the outer situation develops into a deep love relation that the woman may put all she has into it. But to be able to carry herself in either a light or a serious erotic attachment, she needs to be whole or on the way to it, and, hence, to be connected consciously with her own animus.

We have come through an age of wild experimentation in the erotic sphere as elsewhere, and many young people have become the victims of a movement they do not understand. An inexorable process in the unconscious was breaking up the old tables of value and clearing the way for something new. It is not possible to be objective in viewing those times, especially when we ourselves may have been the pawns of the Zeitgeist. But I think we could also glimpse the emergence of a new sexual morality, whose object includes the development of the whole person, rather than demanding the imposition of ready-made standards. This releases men and women from rigid and arbitrary external rules. Some may get hopelessly lost, but others will explore in freedom the real meaning of the experience.

If the patriarchal laws are being relaxed, those of the Mother become all the more necessary. Here the criterion is the way a thing works, toward growth or decay, integration or disintegration, love or identification, the Self or dissolution in the collective. Success or failure in finding these laws determines the fate of the individual and perhaps also of the entire human race.

3
Marriage

Much of the material relevant to marriage has already been given, for it is really a special case under the general heading of men and women. But it is also unlike any other relationship, for not only does it aim at permanence, it is an accepted institution, a part of the laws as well as of the mores of the community. It is therefore not just a matter of individual happiness or individual morality and psychological development, but, in our civilization, the basis of society.

The home is the fundamental social unit. The well-being of the community depends upon the soundness of many such units, which in turn require large commitments from the partners who form them. These vested interests are to some extent protected and involve legally recognized rights and obligations on both sides. But, of course, the paramount stake that society has in the institution of marriage is the children who constitute the future promise or doom of the community. No man can live unto himself alone, nor can the social implications of the relation between a man and woman be evaded by any couple willing to accept the whole of the experience.

Indeed, perhaps there is no better measure of the nature and importance of such a relationship than the facts and attitudes revealed by the answer to the question: Does this mean marriage, and if not, why not? This matter used to be taken care of by Papa with his stern question, "Young man, are your intentions honorable?" But these days Papa is usually cordially invited to keep out. Yet the young people often do not deal with this important problem adequately themselves. The result is that they are liable to stay too long in a sort of provisional living or else take the leap without due consideration. Not infrequently a patient has told me about a love affair in which both participants had been drifting quite long enough, but nothing serious had been said on either side. Neither knew where the other stood. So I have brought up some pointed questions to clarify the individual's own attitude. Let us take a case which is actually a good average and can represent many others like it.

The patient is a woman. I ask her if she loves the man. She thinks she does. Would she like to marry him? There she is not so sure. He is Catholic, she Protestant, and she does not know whether he would insist on having all the Catholic rules observed in the home, such as those concerning contraceptives, the bringing up of children and so on. She does not know his income, whether he could support a family, or even whether his attitude is responsible enough to undertake one. Then I inquire whether he wants to marry her. Again she does not know. There is no Papa to handle the situation and she has no idea how a woman can go about finding out without seeming to be asking him to marry her. So the only alternatives appear to her to be either to go on drifting even though it has become a real problem to her, or to be the one to propose and so risk scaring him off completely before the real issues have been touched.

Of course, this dilemma is the result of an animus assumption if she is really seeking to find the right way and not to coerce the situation, but it paralyzed her just the same. That is exactly what the animus seems to want to do in such a case. So I call her attention to the fact that neither of these alternatives truly represent her real feeling. She "thinks" she loves him, but that very expression shows she is not certain. The uncertainty lies in the still unresolved question whether her involvement is love or an emotional infatuation for a projected animus, so naturally she does not know which way the road is meant to go. This realization releases her, for she sees that her desire is truly not to get him to marry her but to discover the meaning of the important bit of life between them. So the next time he makes love to her she reacts frankly in the spirit of the moment. She says something, "John, my dear, where are we going? This lovemaking is getting too much for me to dare go on playing along in the dark." That leaves him perfectly free to draw back in consideration of her feeling, or, if he wishs, to declare himself so they can begin to talk in the open about their relation to each other and the adjustments that marriage would involve, and in that way try to discover whether the light is green or red for a deeper relationship.

The problem from the man's side, if he really wants to consider marriage seriously but is not yet ready to propose, is no less difficult. Whereas she is afraid of saying something unwomanly, seeming to be trying to catch him, he fears to get caught prematurely by giving the impression that he is proposing, when he really wants just to explore the way together. The conventional attitude of gallantry expected of the lover adds to his difficulties. How can a fellow propose and then lay down a whole string of conditions? But if he will freely commit himself to his love as far as he can, it will then be possible to talk about the realities they will have to meet because of differences in tastes and ways of life, as well as the very material question of whether she can make do on his income, what it will mean compared to what she is used to, and so on and so on. It is in talk like this that the distinction emerges between a temporary infatuation, in-loveness, and the possibility of a real individual relationship.

But marriage is not usually thought of in these conscious terms. If it is not a case of blind falling in love, it is apt to be worse, a matter of ego calculation alone: Do I want to be married? rather than, Do I love this man? I had a very amusing experience in this connection when I was a young doctor doing general practice. I was called in one day to see a woman just over thirty, the mother of seven or eight children, all under ten years of age. She was simply worn out, with no more strength or resilience in her. She said wearily, "Never get married. Never give up your freedom. If you do you'll only regret it once and that will be all the rest of your life." A week or two later I was called to treat a schoolteacher, fiftyish and a spinster. As I got up to go, she said, "Young woman, I like you. I am going to give you a piece of advice. If he is at all a decent chap, take him before it is too late! I've lived a long time and I know."

Well, whatever you do, you must pay for it. The point is to pay for what *should* belong to you, not for an imaginary value or an escape from the inevitable dangers of living.

An essential of the marriage relationship, according to Keyserling, is the acceptance of a common fate.[41] It means that a man and woman go hand in hand to complete each other through all the various experiences and vicissitudes of life. What happens to one affects the other; where one is stricken, the other is ready to help; the home and the income and the children are held jointly, and a piece of good

---

[41] Count Hermann Keyserling, "The Correct Statement of the Marriage Problem," in *The Book of Marriage* (New York: Harcourt, Brace and Co., 1926), p. 9.

fortune is a gift to both. The marriage vow pledges to love and honor, if not to obey, "till death do us part."

People often ask how it is possible to promise to love and honor, let alone obey. Is there not an element beyond voluntary control here that makes a mockery of the words? Personally I think the true spirit of the pledge, if it is interpreted psychologically, has as much meaning today as it ever had. For anything the human being can promise must always carry the proviso, *Deo concedente*, God willing. The promise means then to leave no effort or means of which the partners are capable untried before breaking the marriage. This carries a full commitment and may require real inner discipline, for, when a serious difficulty or a strong counterattraction comes up, there may be a tremendous centrifugal force against which it is hard to struggle in these days when external rules of conduct are no longer considered to be binding.

A woman once came to consult me with the actual, though unexpressed, purpose of getting my moral authorization to seek a divorce. You'd be surprised how often people come to an analyst to get scientific backing for something they are quite certain they never could get a religious authority to approve. Well, of course I wasn't giving her any, but tried to help to clarify her motives. She was sure there was no question of her husband's faithfulness, nor was she interested in another man. She said her husband was quite all right. "But," she added, "I'm just not in love with him any more." She admitted he was most kind and considerate (probably too much so, I thought); he did not stay out nights and was what is called a good provider. "But I'm just not in love with him," she kept saying. I tried to get her to see that hers was by no means an uncommon situation after a few years of married life, and that it meant a basis of greater mutual understanding should now take the place of the original being in love. But when she found that I would not collude in what she wanted to do, so that she could do it without having to think ill of herself or put herself in the wrong with her husband and the community, she soon dropped off and that was the last I saw of her.

In another case the partners' reluctance to put their best into saving the marriage was rather more subtle. The husband was a very intelligent man with an intense, sometimes violent nature, capable of making strong anima projections in which he was tremendously demanding upon the woman. He had married an attractive girl whose emotions were securely tied up and neutralized in an uncongenial family situation. Here was the fuse and the dynamite. There were soon difficulties between them, which they could meet only by quarreling and an increasing coldness on her part. His more intense nature made him selfish and exacting from her point of view; she protected herself by withdrawing more and more into her shell and immersing herself in the care of the children. He was being analyzed and begged her to do so too, but she did not feel the need for herself, and did not want to come over so far to his side by accepting his course of action.

Then the inevitable happened—he fell deeply in love with another woman, who returned his feeling with all the warmth he had missed with his wife. Moreover, she *was* interested in analysis, and, in consequence, could meet him with a frankness and a degree of consciousness which were meat and drink to him. But—he was fond of his wife in spite of their troubles, and loved his children dearly. He made up his mind to be frank with her and to implore her once again to go into analysis, which, roused by this bombshell, she was now glad to do. Perhaps he had some feeling that the analyst would take care of the situation in case he decided to ask for a divorce. He readily agreed, however, to my suggestion that he postpone any such drastic action for a year, and in the meantime do what he could to make it unnecessary. Then he dreamed:

> I am at a meeting of some sort in an unspecified place in Europe. Jane [his new love] is with me. I leave to put a man, who is also myself, on a steamer that is sailing for home. First I take his valises, and then come back and get him on board. The steamer is one of the stuffy respectable tourist sort that are "preferred" by impecunious professors, who claim that they "like that way of travel."

Here you see that his real libido, represented by himself, is far away across the seas and he is sending back to the home situation only a piece of his shadow. This fellow is "impecunious," that is, lacking in free libido, and is content with a stuffy commonplaceness half concealed under the pose of not caring for material values. All this is indicated by the rather contemptuous description of the steamer on which the shadow-figure "preferred" to travel. But the dreamer is a man of integrity and realized from the dream that he had to play fair for the year of trial and do the best he could to meet halfway any changes in attitude that might bring him closer to his wife.

The wife began with dreams of a journey to be taken, but without any indication of a serious purpose. They were hardly more than a restless drifting around. In one, she attended part of a college course with a friend, but when she was expected to take the examination she had made no preparation to enable her to pass. However, the professor said it didn't matter, and for her to come to see him at his home.

You see she is late to the course, for her husband had been urging her to be analyzed for a long time before she made up her mind, and, even at that late date, she does not realize that the acid test of the marriage, the examination, will surely come to show whether she is properly equipped or not. In the dream the father animus, in the person of the professor, interposes between her and reality and saves her from the consequences of her negligence by making her his special pet. As a result reality does not touch her and she can go on giving a beautiful example of the provisional life. There is always a cushion of nonrealization between her and hard facts. She simply assumed that *her* marriage could not break, so she never made the final commitment or the final effort.

This was followed by another dream of an examination, but this time she herself had taken the whole course (she had accepted analysis as necessary for her in this crisis). But again she had not done any real study for it and felt she would surely fail. That is, though she had submitted to her need for analysis, she still is not willing to do any work on it herself and the animus now justifies her resistance by a pessimistic outlook upon the possibility of success. The examination is a sort of initiation ordeal; it corresponds with the serious situation that confronts her in her marriage, where also she is being tested and finds that she has done nothing to consolidate a real relatedness with her husband. She has done all the things she had been brought up to regard as part of a wife's duty, but on the affective side she had been like a sleepwalker, going through the motions required by the social institution of marriage. It had never occurred to her that her husband needed more than the company of her mere persona, or that a relationship which was not kept alive and vital every day would soon wither and die.

I tell this story not because it is unique, but because it is, with variations, so terribly common. With only slight changes it could apply to many couples I have known. In this case the partners wanted to do the right thing by each other. The trouble was that they were both unconscious on the eros side. Also, the wife's resistance to analysis because it was the husband's way had kept her from getting the help she so sorely needed until almost too late. It was said in the previous chapter that when a marriage is in difficulty, it has a much better chance to be salvaged if it is the woman rather than the man who comes to analysis. This case clearly illustrates the point and also the significant fact that marriages ending in divorce practically always break from within, even when it looks as though the cause is an outside infatuation. There may be erotic attractions to others, but in a good marriage they can usually be weathered.

Sooner or later the hidden difficulties between the partners are certain to come to the surface. Almost anything may be the occasion, another love or a particularly heated quarrel or a financial disagreement. The infection cannot be healed until it has come to a head and then only can the poison be drained. The resulting crisis may explode the marriage entirely, or it may lead to the redeeming changes in the partners that will make possible a new start on a far sounder basis.

A few generations ago this stage would have had a much better chance of remaining innocuous, just a passing phase, for then marriage was more generally accepted as a sacrament you had to put up with, if humanly possible, as a matter of duty. Or, if you were not religious minded, at least it was a convention which could not be infringed without involving yourself and family in an unpleasant scandal. Sexual affairs outside were frowned on and even divorce was considered a matter for shame. True, you might dally with another and still, to all intents and purposes, be a pillar of the church, but it had to be done secretly and on the side, and, if suspected, social ostracism would be the result. But today there is less loyalty to the institution. People in general expect more of marriage, something more personal and more satisfying. Whether this change is good or bad from the psychological point of view depends upon what people seek instead. Some would put it that they expect personal happiness if they are to remain faithful to a relationship, or even to stay in it at all. Others would say that they must be faithful to an inner truth that cannot be put into any institution or formula, but is a definite experience. So now, when "the time of troubles," as Toynbee calls it in the case of nations, arrives, the fate of the marriage depends upon its quality and the attitude of the partners. Usually it will have to come alive or die outright.

In my experience, it is not a rare occurrence that an extramarital affair may be the thing which jolts a marriage out of the treadmill it sometimes becomes. It is certainly a kill-or-cure treatment and emphatically not to be advised by the analyst; yet it may work. There is a novel which appeared some years ago, *God's Counterpoint*, by J. Beresford, that illustrates this so dramatically that I will outline the story, for these little glimpses behind the scenes of life, either in reality or as seen with the insight of the artist, widen one's experience and understanding.

The story is about a man married to an attractive and devoted woman. At first they were very much in love, but soon he began to have trouble in the sexual side of the relation. He had been puritanically brought up, and, to him, sexuality was just an animal lust that did not seem to belong in the same world with the woman he adored and put on a pedestal. The result was that he became impotent. Their relation had been one of in-loveness rather than one having the possibility of individual communication, and this difficulty of his made an intolerable situation between them. He felt humiliated and retired into the solitude of his own study, where he was unable to accomplish anything; he spent his time in morbid introspection, with terrible feelings of inferiority. That, of course, led to jealousy of his wife. He could not bear to have her leave the house, for he was tortured by the idea that she was meeting some other man. He did not even like to have her be with her women friends, for he thought they talked about him. If he saw her laugh, he was sure she was laughing at him. She really had loved him enough to have been willing to forego the sexual side of their relation if necessary, but she could not bear his complaints and suspicions that were worse than an ocean separating them.

After months of this, a cousin of hers, a woman who had lived most of her life in Paris, came to visit them. The wife had been reduced to the depths of unhappiness without a word to another soul about it, but now she decided she must talk to someone and she took this opportunity to make a confidante of her cousin. The latter listened to the whole story most sympathetically and then said, "Come now, you can get him to perform if you really want." The wife, who was much less sophisticated, said she had tried for months without making the slightest headway. The cousin replied carelessly that she'd risk a bet that *she* could do it all right. The wife was desperate and answered that, though she still loved him, the other woman had her permission to do whatever she liked.

In spite of this liberality, which was really based on pure skepticism, it was a great shock when she came down to breakfast a few mornings later to find a note from her husband saying he was leaving home with the cousin, for good. He asked her forgiveness, and that was all. She was now more alone than ever, with not a soul she could talk to. But she was courageous and turned to the dreary attempt to make what she could of a life from which all the blood seemed to have been drained. Months passed and everything still reminded her of her husband, so she was not surprised when a man coming down the lane one day while she was working in her garden seemed to have a resemblance to him that made her heart skip a beat. The resemblance was so strong that she could not take her eyes off of him. The figure was so like him; it was his walk, yes, and he was now hesitating an instant at the gate, and turning in!

It was indeed her husband returning home. He told her he had recovered his virility with the cousin, whose life did not invite the projection of immaculate purity, and had gone with her to Paris in an excess of relief from his feeling of inferiority. But as the weeks went by, his thoughts had turned more and more to the one woman he really loved. The cousin had been a wonderful partner in bed, but otherwise there was very little congeniality between them. So at last they had parted, amicably, by mutual consent. He asked his wife if she could ever forgive him for what he had made her suffer.

I need not tell you the rest. His anima had been split, as is frequently the case. On the one side was the virgin mother, holder of the spirituality, and on the other was a low-type harlot who represented crude lust and corresponded to the exaggerated chastity of the former. He simply could not bring them together at the level where he placed his wife. He had to take the risk and go down into the black mud, not knowing what degradation and compulsiveness the experience might involve. This is no pretend danger; it is terribly real, this descent to the repudiated part of the psyche. To a puritanical mind like his, it seemed that if he cast away his "principles," his accepted moral code, there was no telling to what depths he would fall or what disastrous consequences might ensue. But yet he was not entirely irresponsible about it, and so was able to make the essential discovery that the meaning of life, and therefore of a meaningful marriage—indeed a marriage that will work at all—cannot be found by running away from one's natural libido, but by daring to explore and integrate it.

The bulk of mankind in this generation, and perhaps for a very long time to come, will not be able to have a meaningful life in the sense of conscious integration, and one cannot know in advance which persons are the ones who will be called to make the attempt. So the warning not to take away the lifeline of the others by giving rash analytic advice cannot be too strong. Certainly the analyst has to try to clarify the situation of the patient, but not point the way. If the question of giving up the security of conventional morality arises, it involves a fateful moral responsibility. Rejecting the average, collective truth, which works in the majority of cases, and taking instead the crutch of the analyst's ideas, certainly does not lead to individuation but to a hellish dependence. The average person probably belongs on the average way. One of the desert fathers once said, "If you see a young man trying to climb into heaven of his own will, catch him and pull him down, for it is not expedient for him." The necessity to deviate from the collective path must come from within, and from something more authoritative than the ego.

In speaking of men and women in the previous chapter, we saw what heights and depths may be constellated between them. The god and the animal, which Jung has called the prestage of the god, may come very close. But what about marriage, in which the day to day experience of sitting across the breakfast table from each other, working on budgets and accounts, all the shared pleasures and irritations, make a personal routine in which these august archetypes seem to have little place? The intensities of love often enough are exchanged for a more or less comfortable existence and the many advantages of a team over single life. But this banal anticlimax is not inevitable. Or is it?

Well, once again the Kundalini symbolism is helpful in clarifying the psychological situation.[42] It will be recalled that the Manipura chakra, which lies just below the diaphragm, is the fire realm, expressing the passion produced by the clashing of opposites. You may remember it is said to be the place of jewels because of its tremendous libido in flaming action. It is the chakra to which the majority of dramatic plays and stories belong, and, to one who has not gone beyond it, the next step will appear tame and anticlimactic. One cannot even imagine the values of a life too far beyond one's own level of development. Intensity of living has an obvious attraction. But at the stage of Manipura, the human being is unfree and is the helpless pawn of the gods. The individual has not emerged from the veil of Maya, which is the colorful drama of nature. It is only in Anahata, the chakra above the diaphragm, that the first glimpse of Ishvara, the Self, is obtained, appearing in the form of an antelope, and this brings a feeling of illumination, unimaginable below. But that experience is deeply interior and does not make good drama. It is unique, inexpressible, mature; there is nothing to be said. "The Tao that is talked about is not the true Tao." Life at this level can look dull and uninteresting from outside.

So when the original in-loveness wears off in daily married existence, what comes next depends entirely upon whether or not the man and woman have lived through the passionate outcry of Manipura and come to Anahata. If they have, their love will have changed correspondingly and have become a true devotion to the partner, on the one hand, and to an inner experience on the other. The archetype does not cease to exist when it is no longer projected. The mystery of life cannot be sterilized into nonbeing. But now, instead of needing the other person to carry the image, it is felt in the mysterious power of love and life that comes to each through the other. Then Maya, the veil of appearances, is seen no longer as illusion but as manifestation, and the archetype is sensed as an organic pattern of living and not as a cheat.

It is just because marriage is a *long-term* relationship that it demands a continuous process of overcoming the separative egotisms and autoerotisms if it is to be viable and capable of growth. In a mo-

----

[42] See above, pp. 13-14.

mentary encounter it is usually possible to keep the less agreeable sides of the personality out of sight, but not in marriage. One by one they come to light, but here fortunately always with an extra incentive to overcome them. I recall a woman who was not able to make up her mind about whether or not to marry a man of whom she was becoming enamored, because of a snobbish feeling that he did not quite belong to her social background. She said to me, "I just can't decide whether to take him in spite of his being a carpenter." My answer was, "Wait until you can say you marry this man *who is* a carpenter, not *in spite* of it." She agreed to wait, but the very next day she came in saying, "I am marrying John who is a carpenter." And, though I cannot say they lived happily ever after, the marriage was a success. And her snobbishness about him was gone.

In interracial marriages one is apt to find in an exaggerated form the subtle poison of an ego reservation, such as this woman started out with. Where the gap between the respective races is considerable, the psychological problems will be correspondingly serious. If the difference is as great as that between white and Negro, the difficulty will be so great as to be a serious threat to the marriage. It is almost inevitable that some element of befriending the underdog should come in on one side, with an unconscious expectation of appreciation or even gratitude in return. The bill is sent in all sorts of ways, as, for instance, by assuming that the Negro should be the one to make all the necessary adaptations, instead of it being fifty-fifty. And if he or she fails to meet this demand, the repressed prejudice comes out in a poisonous form. Also, while the partner may be accepted, it is a very different matter with other members of the family and friends. And the worst problems of all may arise in regard to the bringing up of the children.

I have spoken of interracial marriages because they illustrate in an extreme form the problems in any marriage involving a difference between husband and wife which has ego values attached, whether due to wealth, social position, education and cultural background, or race. Such unions work best where the individuals are so undifferentiated that these considerations do not matter, or else at the opposite extreme, where the partners are highly conscious, able to meet the difficulties for what they are worth and no more.

Jung, in his essay "Marriage As a Psychological Relationship," points to the fact that each partner will tend to settle into the position of being contained by the other on his or her inferior side.[43] The woman seems more often to be contained by the man on the thinking side (logos) and the man likewise by her on the feeling side (eros). Thus the contained gets the sense of a comfortable womb, which, incidentally, is the only situation in which one human unit is in fact completely surrounded by another. But the price psychologically is a cessation of growth, until the container, whose facets are by no means equally protected by this arrangement, becomes restive and looks around for someone else. That ends the cozy unconsciousness, but it may force a development that gives the marriage a start on a new, more truly related level. But even during the stage of the projection of somewhat flowery images by the contained, there may be a certain stimulating effect on the container, who is cast in a large and potent role, thereby awakening dormant capacities that without this stimulus might never surface. Reality is the great awakener, and the close, long-term association with another human being that marriage involves makes it, for most people, the most effective situation for the arousal and development of consciousness.

Before ending this discussion I must say a word about the fashion among quite a number of people these days to agree that neither husband nor wife should give up the freedom of association with the other sex, but should be at liberty to have whatever affairs seem desirable, with no grumbles from the partner.

The idea is that we should be realistic enough to accept human nature or the libido, or whatever, and place no restrictions on its uninhibited expression. They quite forget that restrictions are natural too. That was the mistake Freud made. Actually, claiming unlimited freedom for the ego does the greatest violence to the true stuff of human emotions. It is a terrible disparagement of their importance in life, as well as their power for good or ill, to assume they are merely a matter of pleasure for oneself or of polite consideration toward the other person. I have never seen an extramarital erotic relation that had no effect, one way or the other, on the marriage, if it was really alive.

---

[43] *The Development of Personality,* CW 17. [For an extended discussion of Jung's essay, see Daryl Sharp, *Getting To Know You: The Inside Out of Relationship* (Toronto: Inner City Books, 1992).—Ed.]

Those who are glib about offering unlimited freedom within the marriage usually imagine that any outside situation will be light, if not actually trivial. They forget that something deeper than conscious intention will have the last word here. It is useless for the rational mind to say to a process of nature once set in motion, "So far shalt thou go and no further." At any moment a chord may begin to vibrate deeper than any the individual has experienced before. Unless, of course, the affair is utterly cheap and meaningless. But the cheapening of the erotic life is as great a threat to marriage as a powerful rival. The person whose sexuality is lived for personal gratification outside the home is sure to bring a bit of the same attitude back, to the great disadvantage of the marriage. The cynicism of a wife who is willing to accept her husband's marital deviations so long as he doesn't *love* anybody else will sooner or later be discovered for what it is—a bare-faced proprietary claim that rejects his right to decency with any other woman.

But what then is the alternative? If the offer of complete sexual freedom boomerangs, is the answer to be found in strictly enforcing a monogamous marriage, with no possibility of sexual experience outside? There are many people who are not content with solutions that depend upon the imposition of rigid rules. Those whose religion gives them a satisfactory answer do not have to face this problem. But for the rest of us, I think the only hope of avoiding chaos is to find the law of the Self within. There is a morality without formal rules. The point then, as Jung has so often said, is not what one does but who does it. Following the rules doesn't make morality. The most terrible acts may be committed under the wing of holy matrimony. But an attitude of "the devil take the rules, I'll live as I please" is worse. Nietzsche writes in *Thus Spake Zarathustra:* "Free, dost thou call thyself? Thy inmost thought would I hear, and not that thou hast cast off a yoke. There are many who have thrown off their last value when they throw away their chains."

Those who discard the old laws and mores that embody the collective wisdom of generations and attempt to steer a solo flight will meet the fate of Icarus or Phaethon and crash to earth, unless they succeed in following a superior inner wisdom, a wisdom they do not even know in advance, which applies only to oneself and at the moment, and whose guidance one must daily seek anew. Then it may be possible to recognize the value of a single permanent relationship, and at the same time to realize that one cannot preserve this by arbitrary standards but must grow up to it, if that is the choice, by the serpentine path of each day's honest effort. Then the freedom one takes is not for the ego, but arises from an unshakable loyalty to an inner center. To this one sacrifices not only the protective authority of collective morality but the willful ego even more. And, to quote Emerson again, "If anyone imagines that this law is lax, let him keep its commandment one day."

Not every couple is capable of making a permanent relationship, much less a conscious one. All too often there are incompatibilities that cannot be bridged, differences of temperament that preclude understanding, and, worst of all, qualities in one or both that make life simply unbearable for the other so that divorce seems the only remedy. Even then it is sometimes possible that the offending party may be able to change, with or without psychological help, or the other may become less critically sensitive. I once heard a man who had been amicably divorced, and later analyzed, express the opinion that most divorces are ghastly and unnecessary mistakes. However that may be, I have found in my own experience that anyone, especially a woman, who does not take the preservation of the marriage with the utmost seriousness will not be really serious about anything, unless it be the quest for pleasure or power.

There certainly is such a thing as Jung has called the "infantile lust for freedom," by which he means freedom for the headstrong and self-indulgent ego to function without restraint. But naturally this is only a childish blindness. There is no such thing as unlimited freedom for the ego. Every choice has its inevitable price. Even your reading this book at the moment is at the expense of every other possible use of the time and perhaps the money. Nietzsche has said that the moment of choice is man's creative opportunity. This creation is of one's life. Inevitably the unbridled freedom of the greedy, immature ego means the sacrifice of all the values tending toward maturity and completeness.

So must we consider freedom of divorce. Whether it is a renegade move or not depends upon whether, after everything else has been tried, it is the expression of a self-centered individualism or a true and necessary defense of the individuality. In the first case it will lead toward personal and social disintegration, in the second toward more creative, fuller living through a responsible allegiance to the deepest sense of personal values.

I have not dwelt on the deep contentment that may be afforded by home and family life, on the companionship of the partners through the years, the renewal through the growing children, the center for friends, the security for all in the midst of the vicissitudes of fate. This is all quite familiar so I have concentrated here simply on some of the psychological processes that underlie the picture, and the growth or shrinkage of consciousness through the experience. In the discussion of the family, I mentioned the archetypes that powerfully influence the relation of parents to children and vice versa, so I will not repeat that here, though it is a part of married life.

Au fond, the family is a biological unit and marriage is the social form by which, in our civilization, it is established and protected. Marriage corresponds to a fundamental pattern in our psychological nature, and is the framework determining the success or failure of a large part of our inner and outer experience of life. To one it will be the best fulfillment of the emotional life; to another the graveyard of the individuality. By an understanding of the underlying psychology it may be possible for the human institution to undergo some modifications to fit the needs of the age, while preserving intact its essential meaning. But no one was ever carried to heaven on the wings of an institution, nor shut out because of not having been through it. And the value of the marriage experience to the individual will be as great or as little as the integrity and devotion one is able to bring to it.

4
Friendship

The subject of the present chapter leads to the heart of psychological relatedness as a conscious achievement.

I do not speak here of those instinctive relations which may exist between children, or even between man and dog, where it is mostly a matter of identification rather than mutual understanding, and where the rapport consequently is, for the greater part, a product of nature. A child, for instance, coming into a new environment, asks only, "Are there any children my age here?" And among primitive people the age group rather than a personal congeniality is the all-important basis of association among the young men, who give their deepest loyalty to it. No one need think, however, that such unconscious factors control human connections only among children or in primitive cultures. They prevail in all collective relationships, civilized and uncivilized, today as well as in times long past.

When I speak of a psychological relationship, I mean one in which there is not only affection but understanding too, and a serious attempt to become aware of the real nature of the libido constellated in the situation, such as shadow reactions, hidden or half-admitted personal motives, complexes that may distort, type differences that may becloud, and archetypal patterns that may influence the mutual feelings and reactions. This effort to become conscious in the living situation is important in order that communion may be released from needless interference and the relation may thus attain its full potential of development.

The chief values that may result are clarity and the liberation of feeling on the extraverted side, and the enlargement of the area of consciousness on the inner. In friendship it is not primarily the unconscious drives that draw people together, and consequently archetypal energy is less dominating and there is a much greater range of voluntary choice. This is in contrast with the relationships within the family and those between men and women, whether in marriage or not. There is nothing here to compare with the great images of mother and father, lover and beloved, husband and wife, parent and child. The primary instincts of sex and parenthood are not an intrinsic part of the situation, except in the case of a homosexual relationship, which will be considered later as a special instance under the general heading of friendship.

I am deliberately limiting the present discussion to the relation between people of the same sex, because in heterosexual friendships the erotic element is certain to play an important part and has already been dealt with in the chapter on men and women. Our present concern is to investigate the facts concerning conscious relatedness, with a minimum of distortion by instinctual and archetypal drives. I realize, of course, that this difference in the various situations is only one of emphasis. I have already spoken of the need for conscious relatedness in the family, in love and especially in marriage, though it should nowhere be allowed to crush or replace the flow of life from the deeper, more spontaneous sources. And reciprocally in a friendship, if it has any depth, various archetypes will be activated and projected, with the stirring of some instinctive reactions. Life is all of a piece, but intellectually we have to isolate and differentiate the parts in order to gain understanding.

Almost any archetype may, under certain circumstances, be projected onto the friend. For instance, a patient of mine dreamed of her friend as a witch. The dreamer was a conventional married woman to whom the idea of homosexuality, whether overtly expressed or not, had been anathema. The dream showed her friend, clad in a dark red hieratic robe, standing at the foot of her bed, gazing at her with a glittering hypnotic eye. The dreamer was feeling the uncanny spell of an erotic attraction, which she both longed for and feared. But the two archetypes which seem most to belong, to have the most organic connection with the inner side of the experience of friendship, are those of the shadow, the figure which is the counterpart of the ego in the unconscious, and of the Self, which is the integrated totality of the psyche.

There is no lack of examples of this sort of relationship in myth and history, but they do not hold quite the dramatic and glamorous quality which is so often a part of the love between men and women. However, the fact that this dramatic intensity is by no means always absent is shown by the Babylonian myth concerning Gilgamesh, the proud, ambitious ruler, and Enkidu, a hairy half-animal man. The two became such fast friends that on the death of Enkidu the whole course of life was changed for Gilgamesh. It is written in the ancient tablets:

Gilgamesh for Enkidu, his friend,
Weeps bitterly and roams over the desert.[44]

And this bitter loss so moved him with the fear of death that he made his epic journey to the underworld, seeking the herb of immortality.

Here the shadow quality of one of the friends, who carries the instinctual vitality, is obvious. Similarly, there is the Winnebago myth of a pair of twins whose names, Flesh and Spirit, make the symbolic meaning clear enough. In a series of adventures Flesh gets Spirit into all sorts of trouble, but in the end it is Flesh who saves Spirit. Then again, in the Faust story—I do not know whether it should be called a friendship or not—certainly Mephisto is the shadow companion of Faust.[45]

The shadow, as we have seen, should not be taken as an exclusively negative figure. For though it has to carry all the dark side of the personality which is rejected by consciousness, and usually the part connected with the inferior function too, it must be remembered that this is the vital stuff, which, in alchemical language, when transformed in the retort, makes the Philosophers' Stone.

The first step in the development of the unconscious potentialities that may be hidden in the shadow is often made possible by their projection onto a friend of the same sex. Here they at least come into view in the same room, even though seen as if in someone else. But there is then the possibility of the assimilation of the projection.

A good illustration of this sequence of events is the story of a young girl of about eighteen. She was born and grew up on one of the most drab main streets in the Middle West. The houses were ugly, the furnishings ugly, people's clothes ugly, and social life bare and banal. She was sensitive and intuitive, and passionately loved

[44] Alexander Heidel, *The Gilgamesh Epic and Old Testament Parallels* (Chicago: University of Chicago Press, 1949), p. 64.
[45] [For a detailed psychological perspective on the Faustian drama, see Edward F. Edinger, *Goethe's* Faust: *Notes for a Jungian Commentary* (Toronto: Inner City Books, 1990.—Ed.]

the beautiful as far as she was able to find it. One summer a woman, ten or more years older, came to town to spend a month or two. Actually, she was a rather phony Greenwich Village artist, but she was a sophisticated, unconventional Bohemian, and she stood for all the exciting freedom and beauty the girl was starving for. Naturally a friendship, based on a tremendous transference, sprang up, and when the visitor returned to Greenwich Village in the autumn the girl went with her and took up the serious study of art. Later, to her great joy, she became quite a good artist and the friendship died a natural death. When the projection holder was no longer needed because the girl was in possession of her own abilities, both for painting and for life, there was nothing much left in the relation. But it had served its purpose of strengthening her confidence and bucking her up to make the break for freedom. For a time, a rather shoddy woman had held the precious image both of the shadow and of the latent creative powers whose origin is in the Self.

In dreams, too, the shadow often appears in a positive form as the companion, the *synopados* (together-goer), the *Fidus Achaetes*. Some typical beginnings of such dreams are, "I was climbing a mountain with my friend," "My friend and I were on a sea journey," "My friend brought me an ancient book," "My friend and I were at a party." Sometimes the action is between the dreamer and the companion; sometimes they are merely together in whatever is happening. When the figure is negative, that fact is an important problem for the dreamer, requiring her to deal with her own dark side and so release her life-and-blood friend from the projection of it.

A person, especially one among one's close acquaintances, may do very well to represent the shadow, positive or negative, but is not a suitable symbol for the Self, for it fails to express the mystery and strange paradoxical oppositeness of the unconscious component. Yet it may do or say that thing which, at the moment, speaks to the dreamer for the Self.

There are two very beautiful examples of friendship that occur in Biblical history. The first is that of David and Jonathan. David, it will be remembered, was a poor boy but a favorite of Saul the king, when his friendship with Jonathan, the king's son, began. Saul, in his fits of madness, turned against David and repeatedly tried to kill him. Jonathan could not believe it of his father, but, when it was proved to him, he was utterly loyal to David. It is said, "He loved him as his own soul." They both took the vow, "The Lord be between me and thee, and my seed and thy seed, forever." Then David had to flee. He gathered quite a following and though he had several good opportunities to take revenge upon Saul and slay him, he steadfastly refused to do so. Finally Saul was killed with all his three sons in a battle against the Philistines. In deepest grief that has echoed down through the ages, David made his great lament:

> The beauty of Israel is slain upon thy high places: how are the mighty fallen! . . . Saul and Jonathan were lovely and pleasant in their lives, and in their death they were not divided: they were swifter than eagles, they were stronger than lions. . . . How are the mighty fallen in the midst of the battle! Oh Jonathan, thou wast slain in thy high places. I am distressed for thee, my brother Jonathan: very pleasant hast thou been unto me: thy love to me was wonderful, passing the love of women. How are the mighty fallen, and the weapons of war perished! (II Sam. 1:19-27)

The other Biblical friendship was that between Ruth and Naomi. That story too is familiar but so beautiful it is worth hearing again. Naomi and her husband and two sons had gone into the land of Moab, fleeing famine in their own country. The sons had married Moabite women and then all three men had died. Naomi resolved that she must return to her old home and urged her daughters-in-law to go back to their mothers' houses, where they could again get husbands. Both wept and at first refused, but Naomi insisted and finally one daughter-in-law sorrowfully agreed. Not so the other, Ruth. Her words of unshakable devotion move us still today:

> Intreat me not to leave thee, or to return from following after thee: for whither thou goest, I will go; and where thou lodgest, I will lodge: thy people shall be my people, and thy God my God: Where thou diest, will I die, and there will I be buried: the Lord do so to me, and more also, if aught but death part thee and me. (Ruth 1:16-17)

The kind of love in these Old Testament stories ordinarily belongs between a man and woman. I have not spoken of it as sexual, for there is no evidence that sex entered into it in any overt way. It evidently did have a passionate intensity, so the Freudians would say, probably with some reason, at least in the case of David, that it was psychosexual. Nevertheless, that was not the main point, but rather was almost accidental in a relation whose significant intensity was somewhere else, the sexuality, if present at all, being just a symbol, not a goal in the experience. Certainly David had quite a number of wives and with some of them he showed no lack of physical desire, so he could by no means be called a homosexual. But the women could not satisfy the creative side of him. And Ruth, in her turn, had been married once, and, after the return to Bethlehem, she married again and bore a son, Obed, who became the father of Jesse, father of David. I shall have more to say about erotic friendships later, in the discussion of the meaning of friendship.

One of the most perfect pictures of an incident between a man and his shadow occurs in a long short story, *The Secret Sharer,* by Joseph Conrad. It is the tale of a young sea captain who has just been given his first command, a sailing ship in the South Pacific.

The first night on board he offers to take the early watch, for he wants the solitude in order to come to terms with himself and his new responsibility. As he leans over the rail looking down into the black water, he sees through the darkness a naked man swimming toward the ship. The man is exhausted and asks to come aboard. He proves to be the mate of another ship anchored in the harbor, wanted by the authorities for the murder of a mutinous member of his crew.

At great risk to himself the captain agrees, thus becoming an accomplice of the murderer, whom he hides in his tiny cabin where discovery is all but inevitable, either by the steward or one of the sailors who come and go constantly with messages. He manages almost miraculously to evade discovery by one of his crew or by the harbor officials during their visit of criminal investigation, and finally puts to sea one night under cover of darkness. In order to let the hunted man escape and swim to shore, if, indeed, he can make it, he takes his ship so close to the rocks that there is angry muttering among the men, one of whom threatens mutiny. Just as the captain is about to strike him down, he suddenly turns and walks quietly off.

He has met his shadow, which is a violent temper, in a situation that is the exact replica of the one which led the man he had kept hidden in his cabin to commit murder. But in his first lonely night watch and in the succeeding perilous days and nights when he gave a place of refuge to that other at the risk of sharing his fate, he won the victory over himself. Now he was up to his job as captain.

As the shadow then, with or without the overtones of the Self, is the archetype which is seen as if embodied in the friend, this projection can cause an identification as close as that of Siamese twins. Then, if the stock of one goes up, the other's automatically goes down, for they balance each other. Where one is superior, the other must at least feel inferior. This leads to the rivalry which is the almost inevitable accompaniment of close intimacy. Sometimes there is a partly unconscious attempt to undercut the jealousy without undergoing the painful process of disidentification, by allotting certain functions to one partner, and others to the other. But both aspects of the psyche are necessary for a growing personality, and sooner or later this reciprocal adaptation will cease to work for one or other of the partners. Unfortunately, this does not usually happen to both at once and a very difficult period may ensue in which the relationship is seriously jeopardized and may go to pieces entirely.

Even if the unfortunate compromise of dividing and parceling out psychological functions is avoided, there remains the bugbear of the jealousy inherent in identification. Can anything be done about that? The only satisfactory answer is, of course, to dissolve the identification by each individual's finding and being content to work within his or her own boundaries. Then the conflict caused by the external situation will only be an added spur to get on with the one enterprise that really matters, the realization of the Self. But this is a very long road indeed. It is the whole of analysis and the whole of a well-lived life into the bargain.

Is there nothing to be done in the meantime, nothing more immediately related to the problem? This is the question patient after patient has asked, and perhaps also the one many of my readers are asking now. I think there are some realizations that may be found along the way on the great journey and are a present help in time of trouble. These may be called the laws of relatedness, or the commands of the Moon Goddess, which is the symbol for the eros principle that Esther Harding uses in her book, *Woman's Mysteries*.[46] I prefer the latter term in talking to people who know what is meant,

---

[46] See above, note 28.

for eros cannot be reduced to anything so masculine as laws, and yet it is possible to indicate the lines that work and those that don't. By understanding these it may be possible to hasten the transition from identification to true relatedness.

Probably the best place to start from is the second of the two commandments that sum up "all the law and the prophets": "Thou shalt love thy neighbor as thyself." This extends to both sides—*yourself* as well as your neighbor. The other pertinent commandment is to "do unto others as ye would that they should do unto you." Our Christian civilization, apart from the teachings of Jesus, has emphasized the part about the other fellow, but Jung insists on both, the creative paradox. In America, it seems to me, it is almost bad form to consider oneself socially. *"Après vous, mon cher Alphonse"* seems to be the rule. Of *course* we consider ourselves just as much as anybody else, but we keep that fact a little dark; we draw a discreet veil over it. The result is that we are too apt to keep it dark from ourselves too, or at least to keep it in a separate, watertight compartment. That means we turn it over to the shadow, with which we often will not be on good terms or even acquainted at all.

But no current will run always outward or always inward. The circuit between myself and the other must be closed. I must receive as well as give, give as well as receive, and both should be done consciously. If people aim to be generous rather than related, they usually turn out to be neither and end up in an isolated complacency. To be sure, if anyone has been a perfect pig, it may be a pretty good idea to try to be generous for a change, for it corrects a previous imbalance and may give a little sense of human solidarity which a cold egoism has forfeited. But generosity has its dangers almost as great as those of selfishness, dangers both to the giver and to the receiver, and most of all to the relationship between them. A giver must be a very conscious person or he will be tripped up by his own camouflaged motives.

One should always ask, "What am I getting out of this?" That sounds horribly egocentric, and actually it is the most unpopular bit of advice, for we do not like to question the motives behind our generosity. But nevertheless it is salutary. Of course, there are legitimate satisfactions in giving. But one should earn the right to give if it is not to backfire. When one loves, there is a strong impulse to pour out gifts, services, oneself indeed, to the beloved. But this is partly due to the inevitable tendency to identification produced by the strong attraction of the object. There is a desire for a complete union, even a merging of the two personalities. And also one is identified with one's possessions, so, in giving them to the beloved, one is actually promoting this merger. A part of myself, the giver, gives another part of myself, the gift, to a third part of myself projected onto the recipient . . . Now one cannot, without dismemberment, have someone walk off with two parts of oneself, so the gifts and services produce an additional claim in the unconscious, and, because unconscious, there is no telling in what terms the bill will be sent.

The secret claim acquired by a generous act is realized with a stark realism in Japan, where there is nothing you can do that is more unpopular than to do a man a favor. For thereby you become his "on man," that is, he is under an obligation to you. If it were a mutually agreed transaction, a loan, for instance, it could be paid off and cease to exist. But a favor creates a debt of honor, without definiteness of size and hence, no matter what you do, it can never be repaid. A Japanese has often been known to bankrupt himself in the effort to settle such a debt, but still the unalterable fact remained that So-and-So had done him a favor. Ruth Benedict tells of a young Japanese boy who wanted terribly to go to an American college.[47] This was before the war. But his father was poor and there seemed to be not the slightest possibility of his wish being fulfilled. However, a kind missionary managed to get him a scholarship and arranged to have him work for his passage on the steamer. He was in seventh heaven. But not so the father, who was furious. He found it intolerable that this foreign missionary had thus become his on-man.

To us this seems like a bizarre exaggeration, but we can understand what the feeling is about. We ourselves, if we are independent minded, do not like to receive large favors. It overweights one side, and so the relation is no longer fifty-fifty. If I make a sacrifice of time or money *for* someone, I am very likely to expect *something* in return, admitted or not.

You can see how this works in a situation where one partner is

---

[47] *The Chrysanthemum and the Sword* (Boston: Houghton Mifflin Co., 1946).

rich and the other poor. The rich one says, and quite honestly believes, "Money means nothing to me, so why shouldn't I entertain often and expensively or give you costly presents, when they mean so much to you?" That sounds like such good common sense that it is difficult to answer. And yet, there may be a trap unless both people are unusually conscious. Sooner or later there comes some delicate point, upon which the mutuality of the relationship hangs, where the rich one uses the sledgehammer: "After all I have done for you, I think you might . . ." This may only be implied, but it is nonetheless coercive. And on the part of the poor one, is it always possible to differentiate the love for the person from the love for what he or she does or gives? And yet in the one case it is object love, with warmth and value; in the other it is autoerotism and cold as a fish.

I have not infrequently seen relationships break up entirely on this snag. Or wealthy people have stopped making expensive gifts because of the experience that their money was loved instead of themselves. And I have also known many independent-spirited people of moderate means who would not accept large gifts, and also insisted that the rich friend sometimes accept the simpler hospitality suitable to the poorer one's own circumstances. A friend of mine once received a bequest affording a modest but comfortable stipend. Being a generous soul, her first idea was to share it with her friends. But they preferred to stand on their own feet. Finally she sighed, "What is the use of having money if you can't help your friends!" She had incidentally discovered thereby the very important truth, that, beyond a certain point of poverty, money really has not much value in producing a good and contented life.

So large gifts of time or money are a quite ambivalent asset in relationships, mostly because of unredeemed areas in the unconscious. With a more conscious relatedness, we become freer to give and to receive. But there are many gifts that we will also no longer care to make. The frequent presents that are an unconscious bribe to gain affection or approval not met by a reciprocal feeling of one's own will drop out. Of course, it is not meant that one should not want one's gifts to be appreciated, but, if there is not to be a secret claim, the gift must be quite as much a service to one's own feeling. Feelings need to be channeled into life in order to be fully realized and integrated. But if the other person does not show any appreciation, the gifts should cease unless one is frankly wooing and gambling on a return. The cessation of giving in this case is not because the motive of the gift was just to catch the other person's libido, but because feeling that is not accepted (note that I say accepted, not returned) should not continue to be poured out, in consideration both for one's own feeling, which does not like to be rejected, and for that of the other person, which does not like to reject.

In addition, the meaning the gift is meant to carry should be made as clear as possible. The famous slogan of the florists, "Say it with flowers," is all very well if "it" is adequately expressed otherwise also. A box of roses may be a man's way of sending love and admiration, or equally well of pacifying the girl he intends to jilt. Such a gift puts out a bait for feeling, while keeping dark the real attitude of the giver. This technique of keeping the victim on the hook, involved but uncertain, may have the most unfortunate results. Flowers, or any other present, should be a sort of obligato accompaniment of a clearer feeling commitment. Otherwise it may be just a trap.

Gifts then (including time and energy as well as money) that are covert bribes, those that are the result of identification, including mothering, and those not acceptable to, or not appreciated by, the recipient, will cease with growing consciousness. What is left?

First, since the important thing is the libido between people, gifts will be merely a language to express it. This means that under ordinary conditions presents will be chiefly symbolic, characterized more by some appropriateness, special meaning or timeliness than by their price. They need not necessarily be cheap, but usually not conspicuously costly either. I had a very good friend, a refugee from Hitler's Germany, who once said rather wryly, "I have had to learn to accept everything offered to me." He was obviously in no position to return in kind invitations or gifts or other favors done him; yet he had no feeling of inferiority for circumstances which were beyond his control. But one always felt the spirit was right; he wanted to do what he could. He would send a carbon of the manuscript he was working on and in which he knew we were interested, or a picture postcard of some subject we had been talking about, and there was never the slightest feeling of obligation between us. The symbolic offerings expressed his feeling and that was enough.

There is another function which gifts of objects or services have in a conscious relationship. This is to meet an emergency, such as illness or accident that takes away the possibility of independence from one or other of the partners. Under ordinary circumstances one may vastly prefer to stand on one's own feet, but if one has pneumonia or breaks a leg or is suddenly bankrupt, then one may well be deeply grateful if there is someone who cares enough to take over the responsibility that one cannot carry. If the bond is close, the other will feel that the fate that strikes one strikes both, one through the body and the other through the heart. In that case, the able one gives, not under duress but because it would be unthinkable to do otherwise. However, if the bond is not close and the need is prolonged, the helplessness of one partner may strain the relationship to the breaking point. In that case, it is really preferable for the sick one to be dependent upon the community where possible, rather than on a friend whose own feeling does not make taking the responsibility a spontaneous choice.

With the growth of consciousness in relationship, the pitfalls in giving and receiving tend to disappear, for the mutual understanding and affection are steady enough for the gifts to have no unexpressed "strings" except those imposed by the laws of relatedness itself. What belongs to one or the other will still be kept clear in order to avoid the danger of identification, but changes in the ownership of things between them will have become unimportant.

There is one other form of giving that should be mentioned, although it is not connected with close friendship but with the collective. It is the subject of impersonal giving to those in need. There are some people in every society who are unfortunate and cannot carry themselves. They are not one's personal friends and there is no individual connection with them. Here it is a matter of impersonal compassion and of loyalty to what H. G. Baynes has called "the human pact." The oneness of all creatures is a dominating reality in the Orient. We have perhaps too little of it. But here friendship itself enlarges our capacity, for it is doubtful whether anyone can truly accept oneself and a friend and not be concerned as well for the wider humanity, of which both are a part. Here again the gift is not out of pure generosity, not just a detached sympathy for the other fellow, but is motivated also by an insistent demand of one's own being. Though we are very far from the Bodhisattvas, who have vowed not to enter into their own bliss until every sentient being has done so too, we nevertheless cannot live at peace with ourselves without stretching out a hand to relieve some tiny bit of suffering in the world. Here the impersonality guarantees the absence of strings.

All this long discussion of conscious and unconscious giving was to clarify the paradox of "your neighbor as yourself" in the basic commandment about relationships. That commandment was second to another—to "love the Lord, thy God" with everything you have. As psychologists we would seek the manifestation of God at the center of one's own being, as the voice of one's own inmost truth, that is, the Self. This, as we have seen, is the reconciler between oneself and one's neighbor, the balancer between thee and me. Without some relation to it, all other relationships have no taproot, no final point of reference, but are at the mercy of one-sided or un-conscious-dominated judgments of the ego. The problem is to bring our human relationships into the lines of force of the psychic center, thus stabilizing them, while at the same time they become part of the larger enterprise of individuation.

The realization of this in the midst of relating to other people gives an Archimedean point beyond personal differences. It may be brought into consciousness by holding in mind the image of a circle drawn about oneself and another about one's friend. It is amazing how many difficulties can be cleared up by this simple image. It helps to clarify the boundaries of each, revealing what belongs in the territory of one and what in that of the other. Actually, I think that among well-meaning people, fuzziness of boundaries is responsible for more relationship difficulties than any other single cause. The circle presents the picture of the relation as being between separate persons instead of an amalgam of the two.

Take, for example, the case of two women sharing an apartment. A brings home an unexpected guest for dinner. Actually, this affects B, for they share the preparation and clearing up of the meals, which in this case would be a little special, and they also share the use of the living room, which would have to be devoted to entertaining the guest. For this reason it is unrelated of A to invite someone in with-out first speaking to B, unless she is sure it would be agreeable to her. In the apartment their circles overlap, so neither should take possession without mutual agreement. Of course, no rule can be rigidly applied. In special circumstances, such as the arrival in town of a close friend, the risk may be taken and the lack of consideration made right afterward. But generally both should have a voice in what concerns both. Otherwise, the circle of one or the other is violated.

Needless to say, there are many people too childish and autoerotic to be able or willing to hold their own desires and impulses in check long enough to avoid infringing the circle of the other person. When they invite a guest, they don't want to bother with inhibiting considerations. But such people are not ready for true relatedness. Whether intentionally or not, when they force the other person to backlog their wishes, it is actually a theft of time and energy and no more just than taking a dollar from the other's pocket. However, the important point is not that such things must never be done, but that they should be done only as far as there is mutual agreement and understanding. Relatedness cannot exist where there is exploitation and invasion of boundaries, and, without relatedness, the closeness of another person is a prison, even when there is an intense bond on both sides.

When one function[48] is so weak as to be only partly usable, the psyche is undefended on that side and illusions and projections troop in and out, bringing insecurity, fear and suspicion. The circle is broken. But instead of working to complete the circumference, the person thus exposed may try to use someone else to stuff up the hole in his own walls. This leads to a death grip on the friend for protection, which may be agonizing for both parties.

This situation is well illustrated by the following case. Two women had formed a strong attachment fairly late in life. One was in her forties, the other early fifties. They were extremely different in temperament, one being a sensitive introvert, the other an extraverted feeling type. It is not surprising, therefore, that they found themselves violating each other's boundaries and hurting each other quite unintentionally, so unconscious claims and resistances piled up. But a strong tie remained between them. Then the extravert dreamed she was telling her friend that she was to be married. This was very painful for her to do and they both wept. It did not seem that she would be separated from the other one by the marriage, though their relationship would be greatly changed. Then she was dressed in a

---

[48] See above, note 23.

wedding gown and veil, but was alone in the church. Feeling cold and forlorn, she took off her veil and wrapped it round her throat. Then it occurred to her that she was not emotionally prepared for marriage and that she would come to me for help. The dream ended by her finding me and there was a warm greeting between us.

Telling her friend she was to be married was an attempt to break the identification between them by getting a superordinated relation to the unconscious, represented by the animus as bridegroom. People are terribly afraid to break an identification, for they can never know how much will be left. It is risking the destruction of something that has held a great deal of libido, with no guarantee something better will take its place. But when one phase of life is outgrown, it simply cannot be retained. If one tries to hold onto it, it becomes poisonous. So the dreamer saw this transition coming and tried to go along with it by loosening the bond that would prevent her from taking the next step in herself. But having done so, she finds that the bridegroom is not there. She is alone in the church, cold, miserable and with the sore throat she had in reality, following a particularly difficult experience with her friend. She obviously is not ready for the union with the unconscious, but this suffering brings her to the realization of her need for analysis, which she immediately acts upon and comes to me. The warm greetings indicate that life begins to flow again in the analytic endeavor.

After three weeks in analysis, she dreamed:

> There was some discussion about the type of cap I was to wear, and finally I saw one such as had been worn by an old man who had paid homage to the young Queen Elizabeth at her coronation. I knew that I was to wear this cap. Then I was at supper with Dr. Bertine, another woman analyst and a young girl. We all sat around a square table. During the meal Dr. B. leaned over and said across me to the young girl, "Here is the answer I should have given you." After the meal I went along a street, much aware of the velvet cap on my head, till I came to the place where two roads met. I chose, without being aware of making the choice, the one to the left, and continued along it.

This dream is somewhat less clear than the first, but I give it because it shows she had found and taken the road to the left, that is, toward the unconscious. She herself is very extraverted, but she has chosen to go by way of the inner realm to seek some help in her relationship problem. The symbol of the cap is fairly condensed. Because of its round shape it is associated to the hat, a symbol that initiated the series of individuation dreams discussed by Jung in *Psychology and Alchemy*.[49] It is round, the form of a mandala, symbol of Selfhood. The animus is now the wise old man, who connects her with the new young queen, an image standing for the barely glimpsed Self. The animus has performed homage to the queen, a suggestion which, as she has acquired his hat—his thinking or point of view—she will follow.

Next, four people are sitting around a square table at supper. The dreamer is one of them, then come the two analysts, one her own, the other closely connected with me also, which hints that this is an analytic communion table, where psychological nourishment is to take the place of the marriage sacrament for which in the previous dream she was not prepared. The young girl is her own immature eros side, who had not been ready for marriage but to whom this short period of analysis has given some directions still unknown to the dreamer. This probably refers to some hint that the shadow, the young girl, receives from me, which the patient herself does not yet realize, "did not hear," but which is likely to become apparent later. People in analysis commonly have the experience of some seed, planted unnoticed during an analytic hour, breaking through to consciousness much later in an entirely different context, or when they are no longer being analyzed and are working along entirely on their own. This will in all probability happen to her.

This woman's dreams show quite clearly how, when her personal circle was being threatened by a close and intense but unrelated friendship, the unconscious did not deal directly with the outer situation but turned instead toward an inner consolidation in the form of an inner marriage. Realizing she was not ready, she went into analysis. The mandala represents her own center to which she is to offer allegiance. When she has to some extent integrated her ego, her young eros shadow and those aspects of herself represented by the two female analysts, she will be able to hold her own with her friend without dominating or being dominated. Her circle will then be com-

---

[49] CW 12, pars. 52ff.

plete but on the first level of integration only, for the masculine side is still absent.

Another image that may prove useful is the idea of the relationship itself as an organism, separate from both the people who participate in it. It is like a plant growing up between them, needing careful gardening from both. Not uncommonly in an involvement, especially between a man and a woman, he will resent some plea she makes, assuming she is making personal demands for herself when she is really trying to save the relationship. An instance of this was a man who demanded that his wife be very economical but refused to tell her what his income was. She saw that he was not cutting down on his own expenditures and felt that, as the one who disbursed the family income, she should know how much it was in order to make the apportionment realistic. But it was very difficult for her to talk with him about it at all, for he always made the humiliating assumption that she was just golddigging. Here money was not the only, or even the primary, issue, but a decent basis of mutual respect for an equal relation between them, the growing plant in their garden.

The same sort of thing can happen in a friendship where the partners are of the same sex. I will give you an example of this, which may seem so exaggerated as to seem highly improbable. But I knew both the men concerned and can vouch for the truth of the story. It happened to an architect at the height of the depression of 1930. Like all other architects at that time he had practically nothing to do. His office, with a large staff, was eating its head off, but he was too kindhearted to dismiss anyone as long as he had a penny left, for there were simply no other jobs to be had.

One Friday afternoon a young friend came to him, asking for a loan of twenty-five dollars. That looked like a lot of money just then to the architect, whom we will call John, and he said so. But the other man, Tom, assured him he would return the loan without fail on Monday. He needed it urgently and could not get a check cashed at the bank until it opened at the beginning of the week. So John somewhat reluctantly handed over the money, thereby going short himself over the weekend.

Monday came, and though he saw his friend, the subject was not mentioned. The same thing happened Tuesday, Wednesday, Thursday, all of one week, and then John, who had not wanted to embarrass Tom, and, as in all such cases, also himself, got up his courage and asked for the return of his money. Tom was most affable and assured him he would have it the next day. John waited, but nothing happened. So a couple of days later, John again brought up the subject. Tom was again reassuring, told him, a trifle patronizingly, not to worry at all, that the loan would be returned all right, but again nothing happened. At last the worm turned and John said he must have the money back that day, or else! Then Tom replied in the most reproachfully aggrieved tone of voice, "Why, I never thought you were the kind of man who would let money come before friendship." The fact that his barefaced dishonesty had long since killed any possibility of friendship apparently hadn't entered his head.

Resistance to the requirements of relatedness is, unfortunately, common to both men or women. But in truth there is no birth without birth pains, whether it is of a book, a painting, a symphony, a human baby or a deep relationship. The fact that it is especially the woman's field is unfortunately no guarantee that she will be willing or able to accept the assignment. But it must be remembered that the way of relatedness, as of individuation, is a road, a process, a journey, and not a completely attainable goal, and the best that can usually be hoped for is to feel truly on the way.

We have seen that the symbol of two circles may be used to clarify the boundaries between one's friend and oneself, which is so essential to the right kind of contact. Now I want to give two or three little practical rules of eros, which I have found to be most helpful. The first is this: *In a relatedness difficulty, react rather than criticize.*

This may sound like advocating a return to an outgrown childishness, for a child reacts just as it feels, whereas a civilized adult has had to learn to control spontaneous reactions. But criticism assumes a superior, objective position from which judgment is passed, whereas reaction reveals your actual state, above all to yourself. You stand without gloves and accept the necessity of getting your hands dirty with the muddy reality between you. Your friend can then meet you as a real person instead of as a judge, a human being who alone and in spite of imperfections is able to make a truly human contact. Pride is sacrificed, but the gate of the heart is opened. Naturally this course of action will not, and indeed should not, be followed by anyone whose deepest motive is not to find the inner truth of the situation and bring it into view. The others will only use it as an excuse for unmitigated autoerotism. For then a decent persona, even if only skin-deep, will make them less of a nuisance to everybody else.

For example, here is a story of a woman who was sarcastically critical instead of reacting honestly. This woman, Mary, shared an apartment with an intimate friend, Jean. Mary also had a boyfriend with whom she was very much involved, though nothing definite had passed between them. However, there had been a misunderstanding about which Mary was greatly distressed and confused. Both girls and the man happened to attend the same dance the next night. He studiously avoided Mary, but somewhat blatantly paid much attention to her friend Jean. Mary was so upset on their return home that it had to be talked about at once, late as it was, and she went about it in a way to make everything irreparably worse. Though she was terribly angry, she did not trust herself to express that at all, but instead said coldly, and with bitter hostility, "Well you certainly did yourself proud with my beau!"

She jumped right in, not as a woman deeply hurt by her friend, but in the spirit of judge and prosecutor rolled into one. The animus had been called in to defend her, and he had aimed at the heart.

Now suppose she had reacted directly and spoken from her feeling, she might have said, "Oh Jean, why, why did you act that way? Didn't you realize the party would be utterly spoiled for me so I could hardly stick it out?" It is quite likely there would have been tears in her eyes had she allowed herself to speak from her feeling in this way. From the power point of view she would have made herself defenseless, whereas in the first case all she was likely to get was a defensive reaction, as actually happened, or else a defiant one. If she had reacted from her heart, she would have brought up Jean's feeling for her, so the rapport would have been saved and perhaps even strengthened. Instead, poor Mary was now at odds not only with the man but with her closest friend too.

Actually Jean was unconscious, but not mean. She was strongly identified with Mary, and without thought or intentional disloyalty she simply found herself attracted by the same people Mary cared for. So when the man paid attention to her, she quite naively accepted it. You can say there was more to it than that, and, of course, there was. There was the inevitable half-unconscious jealousy that identification always produces, which undoubtedly added a tang to being courted by Mary's man. But if Jean had had her eyes opened to the state of affairs, as this situation offered a marvelous opportunity for doing, she would have been horrified, for there was no question of where her major allegiance lay. The man was quite secondary to her, merely an evening's fun. But Mary's frigidly accusatory attitude produced an impasse until Jean finally had an analytic hour on it.

This story illustrates a tremendously important fact. It is this: *The only real yardstick by which to measure the attitude and quality of the partner in a relationship is one's own integrated reactions.* Because Mary had been in the clutches of a cold animus, she got a reciprocal reaction from Jean and did not discover her basically loyal feeling. If Mary had reacted from the heart, there is a good chance Jean would have thrown her arms around her friend in a burst of penitence for her unintentional disloyalty. Trust in each other would thereby have been consolidated instead of undermined by the incident. Similarly, when two people stand on the brink of divorce, it would be well for them to remember that, if the break comes, they will never know whether it was really necessary unless they have previously applied to the relation the yardstick of the most integrated reaction of which they are capable. This means that the reaction of the moment is joined onto the real feeling for the person and for the total situation, so that one is not allowed to obliterate the other.

An integrated reaction is not an exclusively thinking judgment, and certainly not the animus version of it, which usually comes, like the icy criticism made by Mary, from a level far below the head. But it is not just spilling either. A blind emotionalism is not in the least helpful. That would indeed be just a return to childishness. Both feeling and thinking are required.

People often do not realize there is such a thing as eros thinking, a phenomenon particularly strange to men. Feeling so obviously draws people together, while the tendency of thinking is to discriminate and separate, that it is easy to forget that *understanding* is as essential as *liking* in a conscious relationship. Many a woman of the thinking type comes to analysis because she has not been able to slide along comfortably on the surface in her associations with other people, as is so easy for those with adapted feeling. To such a woman it is a great relief to realize that her major function, if she can free it from animus domination, is a great gift, for it enables her to clarify her relationships and to overcome those blockages which, without this understanding, might be fatal. If there is negative emotion present in the situation, it must be accepted as having a place in the picture, for if it is repressed its blackness will be projected onto the other person. But neither should it be given free rein.

In the above situation, for instance, if Mary had reacted merely emotionally, she might have yelled at Jean, "How dare you steal my beau, you snake in the grass!" This hypothetical outburst shows why people generally much prefer to criticize coldly than to put themselves in the wrong by an uncontrolled reaction, the distorted mess of which is all too apparent when allowed to come into the glare of daylight. Here some good thinking is badly needed. Does the man belong to her, Mary should ask, just because she is involved with him? And can Jean be blamed as a snake in the grass for Mary's passionate possessiveness? Granted that Jean was to some extent at fault, does that make Mary blameless? Is not her instant suspicion, in fact, more disloyal than Jean's thoughtless playing around? Had Mary been able to work on the problem in this way it would soon have been resolved.

Before leaving the subject of reacting from one's real feeling instead of putting up a cold barrier of legalistic opinion, there are a couple of points I want to make quite clear, lest what I have said be badly misunderstood. The first is that feeling and emotion are not the same thing. The feeling function evaluates. It says, "I like this and dislike that," or, "This is acceptable and that is not," "This is beautiful or agreeable or in good taste," or the reverse. One can use feeling as a function of adaptation. It is a free expression of one's attitude to something. But a feeling reaction, if it becomes very strong, can readily pass over into emotion. Then the tail wags the dog, and, instead of using it, it uses you. It is a force of nature before which the individual is more or less helpless. Other sides of the psyche also will be drawn into the vortex, but also compulsively. The ego is the victim, the driven, not the driver. So to say, "I feel very badly about something," is an expression of feeling. But a flood of tears or anger would be emotion.

The other point is fairly obvious, but it is amazing how often it is forgotten. This is it: a valid, adapted feeling reaction may be negative as well as positive. It is altogether proper to dislike certain things, even quite intensely. Feeling types are especially likely to overlook this fact and try to keep a situation pleasant, when the reality involves a sharp clash between opposing desires or points of view. Here good feeling would make one courteous (not just polite, which would be nothing but a mask) and truly considerate of the sensitivity of the other person, while reacting strongly to the objectionable point. Pollyanna is no example of differentiated feeling, but of exactly the reverse, for she uses it not to clarify and express true values but to create a make-believe world where everything is lovely. That is pure escapism in a very childish form. Good feeling judgments should fit the reality just as much as thinking judgments.

I do not want to be understood to be advocating under all circumstances the suppression of an emotional reaction, any more than the unconsidered expression of every impulsive feeling. Obviously one does not lightly give up in public one's conscious freedom, as is the case in an emotional state. Indeed, so-called emotionalism is usually due to the intervention of the animus or anima, which is demanding some personal gratification or prestige in a typically infantile way. But powerful emotions, on the other hand, can come from the gods, the forces in the unconscious that are rooted in the deepest instincts and archetypes. These cannot be ruled out or analyzed out of existence by the ego. It is then a question of whether to permit them to show themselves openly or to try to keep them out of sight, where their power is not less but apt to be turned against oneself.

The first class, that of infantile or animus reactions, may be dealt with by such general advice as, "Come now, be your age!" But in the case of deeper emotions, it may be better mental hygiene to go with the wind. Only watch out that it does not carry you over a precipice. In other words, there should always be "somebody home" to be responsible for the acts and words done or said even under the influence of strong emotion. It is a dangerous steed, but the requirement of life is that one should learn to ride it. Or it is a fire, which may bring light and warmth, or destruction. This is the meaning of the fire dances, such as those of the Indians of the Southwest. The participants leap through the flames and carry blazing torches between their teeth as part of a ritual in which they overcome fear by realizing something of the nature of fire in their own being. So whether emotion is to be expressed or dealt with in private, it must be made conscious. If you cannot use it for your own purposes, at least you may be able to prevent it from using you for ends opposed to your conscious values.

I have spoken of two basic rules of relatedness, of which the first is to react rather than criticize. The second is this: *If you want to register a complaint against someone, make it of something specific said or done and not against the personality in general.*

One can change a word, correct an action and apologize for either, but one is what one is, and that is that. One cannot whittle away pieces of oneself to please the world, and certainly should not apologize for them. Though by dealing with single instances the character may change, one cannot make it happen all at once and to order, by a *fiat* of the will or a moral *tour de force*, and so a complaint about what one *is* is a blow beneath the belt. It damages self-confidence and produces a feeling of inferiority which is really wounding. Consequently the reaction is apt to be bitter hostility. It also requires more consciousness in the critic to be specific, for it means that one must come out into the open and allow the real nature of the complaint to be seen. This may reveal the fact that it was based merely upon an unconscious demand. It is one thing to say, "You are a selfish person with no consideration for the feelings of others," and a very different matter to come out frankly with the real complaint, "You took the man I wanted!"

That is an exaggerated example, but it shows the principle. The other person may well have a reasonable defense in the latter case, as one hardly could in the former. One sometimes has to make protests in a relationship, not just in order to get one's due, but, as has been said, for the sake of preserving the good will by eliminating areas of unconsciousness that threaten it. But it should always be remembered that the unconsciousness may prove to belong to the critic instead of to the criticized.

A final suggestion is close to the one about reacting instead of criticizing from a pedestal. It is this: *Do not resent a friend's not doing something you were unwilling to ask or remind him to do, or, conversely, his doing what you were unwilling to ask him not to do.*

Naturally, this does not apply to evil or obviously unrelated acts.

But it helps to weed out many of the resentments that come from un-expressed demands and assumptions about what people should do for you by looking at the way you would feel about them if they were to be expressed frankly. These demands are implied in such cir-cumlocutions as, "I should think he might . . ." or "Why couldn't he have . . . ?"—forms of expression that almost invariably mean, "I think he should have," only it is somewhat camouflaged, so you don't appear, at least to yourself, to be a dictatorial busybody.

For example, suppose you call on a neighbor, taking some garden flowers or vegetables you've grown yourself, hoping thereby to initi-ate a friendship. A reasonable time goes by, according to your idea, without any return. Instead of seeing that your neighbor is either busy or much less anxious than yourself to establish a relationship, you say, "What an unfriendly creature she is!"

In reality, of course, she has a perfect right to choose what she wants to do with her time and the people she wants to be her friends. And even if she is slow in returning your call, her feeling toward you may be good. You could not ask her to come to see you, for you would then have to realize your demand for what you have no right to ask and is of value only if voluntarily given. So, since you have no legitimate claim, resentment is out of order. If instead of making inappropriate judgments you wait quietly to see what develops, it may still work out as you hope, but if not, the cause will not be found in your own power animus.

Indeed, resentment in itself usually means the animus or anima has entered the picture. You may be hurt or angry, you may even dislike the person, all as a conscious reaction to something he or she has said or done. But resentment is like a growl from a subterranean egotism, connected with a feeling of inferiority that cannot or will not come out into the open. So if you find yourself refusing, in the inter-est of maintaining an apparent good will, to say what it is that of-fends you, it is wise to suspect that the fault may not be entirely in the other person.

In the chapter on men and women, two most important character-istics were mentioned whose presence differentiates psychological relatedness from every other form of human relationship. They are mutual acceptance and mutual trust based on understanding. To these two I will add a resulting third, a fairly steady mutual good will. All of them may exist in varying degrees and fleetingly in many other related situations, but the steadiness and reliability belong only in a quite superficial or else a worked-out relationship.

Two people who are in love are certain they have all three, but theirs is notoriously an illusory paradise for they put their trust in something they project. At any moment reality may come crashing in, with a complete reversal of the feeling. Such illusions are back of the familiar statement that love and hate are close together. Only when projections have been assimilated by a long process of development, or at least made conscious to the extent that they can be watched and dealt with, can there be the reality which alone is a secure basis for relatedness.

When the tension between hate, which according to the Hindus is one of the fundamental psychological drives or *kleshas,* and its equally fundamental and balancing opposite, love, has been released gradually by friendly opposition in working out differences, then the libido rises from the Sthula level of appearances to the Suchma level of reality and meaning, where the opposites are reconciled. The meaning of hate is seen to be the separating of the individual from identification with the object, and the meaning of love the union of separate wholes. So conscious or redeemed love is not held in an uneasy balance with hate, but comes from a Self-conscious individual and goes to a known and accepted other. Neither, if rightly centered, is just one of a pair of opposites, but is rather a point of reconciliation of the opposites in an integrated totality. Of course, this is a goal not often fully reached in this lifetime, for such love is the extraverted aspect of individuation. But it helps to keep on the road if it is seen to have a goal, and to realize, even if very dimly, something of what it is like.

Referring again to the symbolism of the chakras, we see that the individual is tossed about in the passionate depths of Manipura, the fire region, by the gales unleashed by the clashing opposites, fear and desire, love and hate, life and death, trust and suspicion. There is great intensity but little freedom. At this level relationships cannot be reliable, for the nonpersonal libido is still in a collective form, appearing as instincts and archetypes only. But when an attitude symbolized by Anahata is reached, one of the archetypal images, that of the Self, begins to assume a central reality. At first it appears just for a fleeting moment—the Hindus say as an antelope in the forest—but bit by bit it becomes the integrating center and the collective forces begin to be reconciled within that individual psyche. The lion and the lamb lie down together as was prophesied, but only because there is a little child, a beginning of Selfhood, to lead them.

This is the great mystery—that out of the often violent interaction of collective forces and the ego something crystallizes which is not collective but individual. And though it is a process in the nonpersonal psyche, paradoxically enough it takes place not in some remote, impersonal realm, but at the very core of one's most intensely personal life. It is frequently touched off by a personal relationship or an analytic transference. And despite the fact that it is a happening in the nonpersonal psyche, the attitude of consciousness does make a difference in the likelihood of its taking place at all. Consciousness cannot do it, but it may cooperate with it. A committed attitude toward the process of individuation clears the way, and every relationship that stirs deep emotion produces a condition in which it *may* happen. For, as we have seen, redeemed love, that is, conscious love freed from projection, is the extraverted aspect of individuation.

Wherever there are projections, some unconscious content that should belong to the Self has been externalized. In the life of a hermit this will not be apparent, for there is no one upon whom to project. But not so where there are close companions. Sooner or later projections will cause difficulty in relationships. Where there is a high charge of emotion, the urgency for a solution is great, but the situation is so explosive that much damage may be done. Where, for instance, the woman is inexperienced and inexpert, and the man fearful and resentful at having the innards of a relation clumsily exposed, only harm may result from talking. No conscious release or new understanding then comes out of it, but instead a permanent wound is left, or the relationship may be wrecked entirely.

But if the relationship is less explosive, and especially if it is between two women, who by the nature of their sex are both concerned with eros, then they are in a position to learn something about the way eros works and how it may be freed from some of the imperfections inherent in the way it is usually experienced. For eros is life as it flows between people, and, as people are never perfect, their experiences will be on their actual level of development. But it is possible that this level may be raised by the greater consciousness which results from sincere work on the material constellated between them.

Now to come back to the three qualities which I think characterize true psychological relatedness: mutual acceptance, mutual trust and a fairly steady mutual good will.

First acceptance. That may seem a strange thing to include here, for you may have the idea that it is implied in the fact of caring at all. But how often do you hear people say, "I like one side of him, but hate the other." Or, "I like her sometimes, but at others I don't like her at all." And for every one who expresses this sort of reaction in words, there are literally millions, including perchance ourselves, who demonstrate by actions that the same is true for them. This shows that it is not a total human being who is cared for (or caring, for that matter), but certain qualities or assets which are expected or demanded as the condition for a friendly feeling.

"But," you say, "how can I love a person's faults?" That is not the point. If you really love, you love the total humanness of the other, which means you accept the faults as an intrinsic and perhaps understandable part of that person. Real love is of a whole and not of a part, except as the part is irradiated by the whole and is an expression of it. One does not love an incarnated assortment of virtues, nor is one's affection graded, like the papers of schoolchildren, according to the excellence of the object. It might be that the choice of the heart would fall very far from the top of the class, but where, somehow, life is willing to flow. There cannot be love, as distinct from transference, without acceptance of the total human being.

The second characteristic of psychological relatedness is trust. Here consciousness is all-important, including some degree of integration of both functions of judgment (feeling and thinking). For one cannot trust with a function which is itself unreliable. A feeling person can easily give credit on the feeling side, but then, when alone, the most awful thoughts about the friend may come up unbidden. And conversely, the thinking person can readily believe in the friend, yet may feel exceedingly uncomfortable about letting the other in on one's own weaknesses. Trust is no easy achievement, except fleetingly, by way of projection. It means that you can bear to have your most sensitive spot exposed to your friend if it has entered into the situation between you. You need to be sure that your weaknesses will not be exploited. Yet, can you assume that anyone, including your friend, has no shadow that might use this knowledge against you? Obviously not. But if both sides are oriented to consciousness rather than to the ego, each will be equally ready to see and work on areas of unrelatedness when they are revealed.

There is no guarantee against getting hurt in a relationship, and trust should not depend on such an unrealistic demand. But if it has proven possible to clarify together the unconsciousnesses that have resulted in wounding the friend, or in being wounded because of an unassimilated complex of one's own, the relationship is enabled to go forward again, and a trust is gradually built up that may be as strong as anything in life.

I had a rather amusing experience in this connection years ago when we bought our two country homes, the summer place on the Maine coast and the Connecticut farm where we spend our weekends. I had two partners then, and we wanted the deed made out to us jointly. When the lawyer heard that we were not blood relations he was scandalized, declaring that the property should be divided, even though we shared its use, for we never could know when the relationship might break up and open the way for all sorts of legal feuds. But we just laughed at that and told him that there was nothing in all his legal bag of tricks half so safe as we were with each other. It was not that we pretended to be able to foresee the future and know that our living arrangements might not change, but we were certain that, if so, we could trust each other to make a decent division of the property. Meantime we preferred to own our homes together.

One woman who had heard me say how important trust is to relatedness bitterly complained to a friend that the friend did not trust her as relatedness requires. This is like saying consciousness is important, so just be conscious. The trust I speak of cannot be given by an act of will and should never be demanded. It is impossible without understanding and reliability of character, but these alone do not produce it. It is, of necessity, the product of mutual experience, or else it does not exist. But there is no right to expect it (any more than there is a *right* to a relationship) nor any duty to give it.

The third characteristic of conscious relatedness is a more or less steady good will. This is not the same as love, which is the gift of the gods, but it may coexist with it. It is rather the result of acceptance and trust, plus a consciously realized human solidarity. In any personal relationship there may be reactions of protest and even of anger, because two separate individuals simply cannot adapt understandingly at every point. Sometimes this will be very painful, for there may seem to be an injurious motive present, such as power or jealousy or possessiveness. Such difficulties are inevitable. But in a worked-out relationship, underneath the anger is a secure certainty that the offense was not intended, and, whether it was present unconsciously or only projected, there is a confidence that it can probably be cleared up and the rapport reestablished on a basis all the more solid. Sometimes, however, all efforts to straighten out a difficulty fail. You feel that you have done your best and that your animus or anima has not gotten into it, but your friend simply cannot or will not meet you on it. Then, if the point at issue is not so serious as to have killed love, comes the necessity for acceptance and good will.

Love that can care only for perfect beings is no more than childish hero worship. A mature person will love the human quality, with its greatness and its limitations, and want to be loved the same way. If some limitation interferes with the rapport for a time, the one who sees further will be willing to take the other as he or she is. This is true acceptance. And perhaps such quiet patience and devotion may finally convince where words could not.

You may have noticed that I have generally referred to the friendship that involves conscious relatedness as being between two women. Indeed, I have wondered whether the men among my readers would not be bored by a subject that probably seems to them to be rather personal stuff. This would be the same resistance in a somewhat different area as that of Eros in the myth, when he insists upon keeping the situation with Psyche a "paradise in the dark." The yin principle moves toward the small, the particular, the concrete case, the personal. But if it is followed through to its essence, we find there its apotheosis, the spirit revealed as the core and meaning of actual living. For where is the Word to be made flesh if not in the life of the individual, which is a quite particular and personal thing?

But men also share in this realm through the anima. Through her it is of the greatest importance to them, but because of her they also fear it. So unless mediated by a woman, they will, in self-defense, try to keep their relationships impersonal. Friendships between men are often strong and exceedingly valuable, but will usually consist of shared thoughts and activities, with very little of an expressed personal nature. Men tend to be related to the idea, to projects and to inanimate objects, where women are related to the person. Women are much more likely to express in words and gestures what they feel about each other. They need to keep a good rapport and will really suffer if it is broken, whereas the man often does not even notice, or if he does he considers it unimportant or boring, and will leave it strictly alone, letting it take care of itself, hoping that by the next meeting all will be well again.

Eugene Henley has rather neatly characterized the difference in the kind of associations men make with each other compared with those between women:

> A man is not much interested in relationship as a rule, but nothing is more important to him than fellowship with other men. Here he feels at home, understands and is understood as a man. He smokes his pipe and sips his beer and tells his stories. Or is silent. He can be silent and nobody seems to mind. A man rates fellowship with his male friends high on his scale of values. It's a primitive kind of association that gives him a sense of well-being, different from anything he shares with woman. Perhaps that's just it. Fellowship promotes an atmosphere of genial warmth, each man being accepted just as he is, provided his standards conform. The men's group doesn't constitute a Society-For-The-Improvement-Of-Each-Other. Nobody wants to change anybody. . . . There's a good feeling of camaraderie amongst men. They're at ease with one another, and that's awfully important to a man.
>
> I think it would be appropriate to state here what I mean by fellowship, as compared to relationship. Fellowship is a participation in collective community feeling and makes no heavy demand on consciousness. Psychological relationship, on the other hand, is the conscious association between mature personalities in which the relationship itself is served by consciousness.[50]

Now a word should be said about homosexuality in friendship. It is not an uncommon concomitant, and, I think, has various meanings. First, I am convinced that by no means all the relationships in

---

[50] "A Man's World," in *Spring 1951* (The Analytical Psychology Club of New York), pp. 71f.

which it occurs sporadically are between true homosexuals, as seems clear from subsequent happy marriages. If, like Freud, you define the type to which a person belongs exclusively by sexual manifestations—anal-erotic, oral-erotic, fetishist, homosexual, etc.—there is no question about it. But if you accept Jung's idea that sexuality is not the goal of the libido, but "the strongest symbol at the disposal of the soul," then you have to seek the meaning of the manifestation in the particular case. Often enough it will prove to be the familiar case of arrested development. The boy may be tied to the mother or the mother archetype and not be able to develop the masculine initiative he needs to make the grade with a woman. And the girl may likewise be mother-fixated and seek to reproduce that kind of relation with someone of the same sex.

There is apt to be an obvious childishness in the attitude of such people toward sexual relations. A man who was accused of seducing a boy protested in a most aggrieved way, "I really wasn't doing anything serious. I was just playing around." That is all sex was to him, just playing around. No responsibility toward himself or the other person, so there was nothing meaningful about it. He was just getting an apparently harmless gratification. This is the attitude of a complete child, but he was a middle-aged man and an extremely gifted one artistically, into the bargain. Women are apt to take the relationship side more seriously. Few care to make casual pick-ups or to indulge in one-night stands with another woman, but the mother-child pattern, the Demeter-Kore archetype, is strong. In these cases, sexuality has come up in the animus, stirred by ideas in the head or a power drive, often compensatory to a feeling of inferiority. But the feminine side is either in the nursery or is identified to the mother. Here we find the greatest dependence and, consequently, the most frightful jealousy.

But not all overtly homosexual friendships are made by pathological or truly homosexual people. There may be real love between the partners, and love is never abnormal. If it is very intense, whether or not for a person of the same sex, it may sometimes overflow into sexual expression. Also, if there is an actual or cultural separation of the sexes, such as exists in the army or non-coeducational schools, homosexual activity may be as natural as it is among cows in a herd that is separated from the bull. Such manifestations are apt to be transitory or outgrown, even if the relationship itself is of a permanent nature. And finally, in these days of general experimentation, people sometimes want to experience homosexuality too, perhaps only from curiosity.

Some educators are terribly afraid of intense friendships among students or faculty. Admittedly there is some reason for this, for intensity is a fire that may readily get out of control. But the answer is certainly not to be found in quenching the fire in a student, let's say, by labeling as perversion what the young person feels to be love. This kind of treatment undermines the student's self-respect and ignores the potentially positive side of the relation, leaving degenerate husks from which only evil can come, evil of perhaps epidemic proportions. However, as long as some educators themselves are such barbarians in the realm of eros, I am afraid these things will continue to happen. If, instead of attacking the particular expression, the student is helped to distinguish between what is really decent and fine and to be respected in a relation, and what is infantility, autoerotism, power, possessiveness and domination, wherever it is found, the form of expression will spontaneously become the best the individual can give. One should not ask for more. I have known plenty of true homosexuals who have avoided overt activity, and nonhomosexuals who have not. But I think that is not the main point. "By their fruits ye shall know them" applies to relationships as well as to people.

I have said that external cultural conditions may affect the prevalence of homosexuality. It is also true that a cultural task coming from the Zeitgeist to either men or women may draw them together with an intensity that can have a sexual expression. I am not now speaking of true homosexuality in itself, but of friendships in which it may or may not play a part. This might be called "cultural homosexuality." In Greece, for instance, when the city state was in process of creation, its development was based on a very close uniting of the men. The relation of the older man and his beloved pupil was all-important, for it was the education of the time, and by it the youth was prepared to carry on and forward the new achievements. The value of these relationships is very frankly discussed in Plato's *Symposium*, from which I quote:

> Suppose there could be a State, or an army . . . made up of lovers and beloved; a better governance there could not be than theirs . . .

and such men, though but a handful, would win the victory, so to speak, against all the world.

In another passage we read that "only they who love will die for others; and not men only, but the women too." In the speech made by Pausanius, it is said that there is not one Eros but two, corresponding to, and sharing, the quality of the two Aphrodites. The elder of these goddesses is the daughter of Uranus without a mother, and so "does not partake of the female, but only of the male; and this love has to do with boys." The other Aphrodite is the child of Zeus and Dione. She is younger and is called Pandemian, in contrast to the Uranian Aphrodite, and hers is the "love that the base part of mankind enjoy, the love of the body. The Uranian Aphrodite on the other hand gives the inspiration of the mind and heart, and will be preferred by superior men." Such erotic friendships held the psychological meaning of that time.

I think perhaps the current Zeitgeist and the genius of Jung together have given to women an assignment and the tools to carry it on with, namely, the exploration of the nature and ways, the implications and processes of conscious relatedness. Here, in the partnership between them, the eros principle of the one may be reinforced by the other, and together they may come to an understanding which would hardly be possible if the area they were trying to explore were opposed by the solidly established attitude of the man. But, as in the myth of Eros and Psyche, consciousness in the realm of eros, though perhaps won by women together, may be of the greatest value both to themselves and, when shared with other women, to others, in helping to improve their more complex relations with men. At any rate, I have had in my practice quite a number of women having close or erotic friendships with their own sex, and the thing they all want is to learn about relatedness. Many are in middle or later life, so they are the successors of the first feminists and are working to clarify the values in that heritage. Of course, they think they come for a purely personal problem, but it seems to me it is a part of the spirit of the time. It certainly had better be, for, if people do not learn to relate more satisfactorily they will probably blow our civilization off the face of the earth.

So we see that, though the archetypes that underlie friendship are not for the most part the numinous ones of the deep unconscious, but those closer to consciousness (except as the resonant voice of the Self is sometimes heard in that of the shadow), still, and especially for women, friendship has an enormous importance, for here she can become conscious of her feminine principle of eros.

A relation with a man constellates a woman's natural eros. The unconscious is activated and she becomes more feminine instinctively. But in a friendship, if it is warm and vital, she may become aware of what is happening. She may become conscious, not by abstraction and logical thought, but in the actual process of living. In an intense instinctive relationship, she gives herself up to the god, projected onto the lover. But when she becomes conscious, she is able to reach out with one hand toward the god and with the other take the hand of the beloved. In friendship, more than anywhere else in life, the ability to communicate is developed. With this comes the possibility of the mutual understanding that can make of companionship or love a true human communion.

Epilogue

In this brief description of relationships between human beings, I have deliberately limited myself almost entirely to the personal side, to the contacts in which one individual meets another in an intimacy sufficiently close for them to make lasting ties and to affect each other emotionally in a way that may deeply influence the lives of either or both.

I realize that a book on the subject of human relationships might equally well include collective relationships such as are to be found in the church, in government, or in business, between employer and employee. But even here a real understanding of these situations depends upon psychological factors which must be studied in the individual in order to discover what makes us behave as we do in a group. Such a study immediately reveals the existence of universal patterns which make it possible to differentiate into types the infinite multiplicity and variety of bonds that may hold one person to another. These types of relationship, such as those characteristic of the ties between parent and child or between siblings or lovers, correspond with the a priori patterns of psychic functioning which Jung called archetypes. We have seen that archetypes are highly charged with energy and, as is the case with the instincts, produce a powerful impetus when they are touched off in some life situation. Hence an understanding of the underlying archetypal pattern is really essential to the understanding of the resulting reaction.

For instance, certain human activities would be totally incomprehensible to a spectator who knew nothing of the sex instinct or the wealth of inherited images that cluster around it. A young child would find such performances hopelessly baffling. Yet they may be a meaningful and organic part of the pattern of instinct. Children and primitives are not introspective and do not see their drives as originating in themselves, but feel themselves to be reacting to the attraction or repulsion of the object. A little boy is angry because his brother got the apple he wanted or scorns girls because "they are silly." He does not realize that, to a grown-up, it is himself that he has revealed and not the other child. In the first case, one sees his youthful greed and aggressiveness, and in the second, his presexual stage of development.

Inner patterns determine our behavior. They reveal our springs of action without our knowing it. But only to those who have reached a stage of consciousness somewhat beyond our own. It is often easy, for instance, to recognize the effect of a father complex upon a man's relation to his boss, making him subservient or rebellious, or of a mother fixation in producing emotional dependence and easily hurt feelings. These examples illustrate the manner in which projections produce an unconscious expectation or even demand that another person should carry some image which is active within, but experienced as if it was, or should be, outside.

It was thoroughly recognized before the work of Jung that the members of a child's family left impressions upon the malleable psyche that often lasted far into adulthood, if not permanently. This effect was considered to be the result of a fixation to one of the parents (Freud's Oedipus or Electra complex), or the persistence of "sibling rivalry" long after the family circle had been left behind. The cure, it was thought, should be the attainment of the attitude of a theoretically "normal" adult, thereby getting rid of these childish ties. But Jung saw that there was a more important factor back of every deeply emotional bond, which often made it unbreakable until the compulsive element was recognized as belonging to an inner content of great significance and was taken care of in a manner more consonant with the development of psychological maturity.

He discovered this while working on what appeared to be an unbreakable father transference to himself in a young woman patient.[51] Here he found that the symbols projected onto him progressed in the course of the analysis in what appeared to be exactly the wrong direction, that is, toward more and more sublime images until the analyst appeared in a form so grandiose as to resemble deity. Then it occurred to him that this was just what the unconscious meant, and that he held an archetypal meaning for the patient that would not yield except by her taking its meaning back into herself and thereby finding in her own inner life the source of that guiding principle which had been represented by him and which had always been revered as

---

[51] See *Two Essays in Analytical Psychology,* pars. 206ff.

suprapersonal, transcendent, divine. Soon after the assimilation of this discovery, the patient was released from her dependence upon her analyst and was able to go her own way with her central value and authority now experienced as belonging within herself.

Of course, it is not only in an analytic transference that these suprapersonal projections occur, as will have become amply evident from these pages. Indeed, Jung has shown that the persistence of a parent fixation itself is generally not due to the strength of the libidinal tie to the person of the parent but to the august images of the unconscious, for the projection of which the natural functions of father and mother offer such a perfect hook. The absolute dependence of the infant is temporarily compensated by the two closest human beings who carry for it those powers one must later develop for oneself. But the ego alone will never be able to meet adequately the more serious of the exigencies of life if it relies exclusively on its own wisdom and strength. It needs guidance from within, less one-sided than its conscious plans and ideas, and it needs a source of renewal and sometimes even of rebirth, both of which it is utterly incapable of producing for itself. These essential potencies in the unconscious come from the archetypes, whose first, and perhaps most moving, symbols are the images of the mother and father. However, it is far easier to try to cling to their reflection in the outer world than to connect with the inner fact that produces it, and this often makes a projection endure until necessity takes a stem hand to aid the will to assimilate it.

In addition to the archetypes of father and mother, I have discussed two other images of far-reaching significance to the personality which are first met with in projection onto another person. These are animus or anima and shadow. Because of its unconsciousness, the beginning of a relationship may be as naive as kittens at play, but if it is to become a real relatedness it will require some serious effort. And this effort must not be the attempt only to be nice and kind to the other person, but to understand both him or her and oneself, and especially the unconscious images that each brings to life in the other. The objective is to clear a bridge, freed from both egocentric distortion and compulsive overadaptation, across which free communication may pass and so permit two human beings to experience themselves, each other and the maximum current of life that belongs in the situation between them. In this way love and meaning unite in a life experience which is not only personal, but also, in a deeper sense, truly religious.

From all of this it may be realized how immensely important, even essential, a part human relationships play in the development of both a satisfactory outer experience and an inner life of vitality and significance. Knowledge of the Self consists not at all of the conclusions formed in autoerotic introspection; it arises in the process of coming to terms with inner forces which we do not invent but discover in a moving experience. It is through conscious relatedness with another person that we may realize the Self. And in a reciprocal action, the Self alone makes real relatedness possible. Or as Jung has said, "Redeemed love is the extraverted aspect of individuation."

Index

Studies in Jungian Psychology
by Jungian Analysts

Sewn Paperbacks